TRANSITIONING FROM PROMISE TO FULFILLMENT

Queen Kirkwood-Hatchett

Scripture quotations from the King James Version of the Bible unless otherwise stated.

ISBN: 978-0-578-05767-5
ISBN: 0578057670

Published by Queen Kirkwood-Hatchett
Printed by CreateSpace, An Amazon.com Company

Contact the publisher for copies of this and other written publications at:

hatchettqueen@yahoo.com

DEDICATION

This book is dedicated to my son-in-law and daughter, Peter and Queeda Keith, my youngest daughter, LaQuilia Graham, my only son, Quintin Hatchett; my grandsons, Quinn Kirkwood, Jeffrey Pierre Keith, and Josiah Keith, who have all shared greatly in my transition and spiritual growth and development.

I also give thanks, praise, glory, and honor to God "...which always causeth us to triumph in Christ, and maketh manifest the savour of his knowledge by us in every place." (2 Corinthians 2:14

INTRODUCTION

According to Miriam Webster's dictionary, transition means "passage from one state, stage, subject, or place to another; movement, development, or evolution from one form, stage, or style to another" (www.merriam-webster.com/dictionary/transition).

In my summation of life, we go through three definite and major transitions:

- Conception to birth
- Birth to physical death
- Physical death to everlasting life

We experience minor and major transitions between conception and death. Transition is a major part of our lives whether we are Christians or non-Christians. If we resist transition, we resist destiny; in contrast, if we embrace transition, we embrace destiny.

Joseph's life in Egypt will be used in this book as the foundation for illustrating transition.

The narrative of the life of Joseph is very remarkable and intriguing while trying to understand transition. It is the perfect model when illustrating the way by which God takes us from promise to fulfillment. In addition, it has all the elements of drama, thrill, prophecy, forgiveness, love, hate, jealousy, passion, drive, integrity, character, patience, life's everyday issues, and everyday family life. Joseph's life in Egypt is a perfect example of transitioning with timely success and it is action packed, full of allegories, and has many symbols, types, and shadows.

Transition is vital to our spiritual growth and development and there is no way out of it as long as we are in our human bodies. We do not know how long we may remain in a particular time of transition, but for sure, no earthly level of transition will last forever. Conduct during transition determines how long it will last. Understanding that transition is inevitable will help us to be successful without getting stuck in the process.

There are **sudden** and **pre-determined** transitions. Listed below are examples of sudden and predetermined transitions.

✓ A woman giving birth to her first child is an example of a predetermined, major transition. Her body goes through many different changes as she transitions from a female with no children to motherhood. Her sleep pattern changes along with her normal day to day schedule. Pattern changes can be very dramatic, emotional, and exhausting. But as time moves on, she finds herself adjusting all the more to the changes. Some women, however, suffer from post-traumatic stress disorder after delivering a child and need severe treatment and support.

✓ Children go through transitions when they mature and leave home for the first time. Whether they are going to college, embarking upon a career, or moving out and away from mom and dad, transition can require major adjustments. For some children, leaving home for the first time can be a very pleasurable experience and something long-awaited. For other children, it can be a very dramatic and unwelcomed experience. Some even end up returning home because of fear of being alone or having to adjust to the transition of adulthood and independence.

✓ Transitioning from single life to married life involves many changes. Living as one means combining incomes and considering the spouse before making final decisions in financial matters; this calls for considerable change. The honeymoon is full of honey, but afterwards, reality of married life sets in and some couples have a problem adjusting to the adjustment. During such time, much prayer and counseling may become the means of survival.

✓ Aging is a transition that many of us do not like to think or talk about; however, it happens if we do not die young. Many changes take place within the body (inside and outside). Living arrangements are sometimes altered because aging can bring on diseases and illnesses that demand residential changes.

✓ Just as we transition from single life to married life, we also experience transition from being married to being single again. Going through a divorce can be a very hard place of transition. It can cause major changes in emotions, self-esteem, income, living arrangements, and can force one into other life-changing adjustments. Maintaining a positive attitude during divorce has an immense impact on the outcome.

✓ Major adjustments are required at the loss of a spouse. Such a transitional adjustment can be traumatic, dreadfully overwhelming, and emotional. Fear may develop due to acknowledgement of being alone for the first time. Trusting God is important, and support from family and friends would be very helpful.

✓ Transition from adolescence to adulthood can be scary as well as confusing. It's the stage in life when the individual is not a child anymore, but not yet an adult. At this stage in life, the body is trying to find symmetry while emotions and hormones are going haywire.

There are normal and abnormal emotional responses to all of the transitions listed above. We are certainly emotional beings and it is quite okay to show emotions when experiencing major changes. Being overwhelmed with emotions, however, can cause anxiety, depression, extreme loneliness, low self-esteem, feelings of isolation, panic attacks, and debilitating fear. Making major choices during overwhelmingly, emotional times can sometimes result in very poor and unwise judgments and decisions. The children of Israel panicked during their transition from Egypt to the Promised Land and began murmuring and complaining about having no food and water. They became fearful and impatient (anxiety stricken) and blamed Moses for a death they had not even died and defeat they had not even experienced at that point. God became very displeased with their actions and they died in the wilderness.

One of the most important determinants of a smooth transition is maintaining a positive attitude. This brings me to the core of the transitional experience.

We will be faced with many decisions, choices, trials, and tests before we reach our destiny; however, just as God was with Joseph, He is with us. He tells us in His Word that "...I will never leave thee, nor forsake thee." (*Hebrews 13:5*).

1

ATTITUDE DETERMINES ALTITUDE

My definition for "attitude" is, "a characterized behavior, whether positive or negative, that responds to an action, person, event, circumstance or set of circumstances."

In the narrative of the life of Joseph in Egypt, Joseph's attitude was one of humility, patience, endurance, integrity, kindness, forgiveness, love, and other positive characteristics. After Joseph revealed his identity to his brothers, instead of exercising revenge for selling him, he forgave them and loved on them.

"Moreover he kissed all his brethren, and wept upon them: and after that his brethren talked with him. (Genesis 45:15)

After the death and burial of Jacob, Joseph's brothers lied to him, saying that their father commanded that he forgive them (Genesis 50:15-17). Did they think that Joseph was pretending to forgive them and was kind to them only as long as their father was alive? Evidently, they did not know very much about Joseph at all. Having a heart like the Christ he had not met, Joseph responded to their fear with these statements:

…Fear not: for am I in the place of God? But as for you, ye thought evil against me; but God meant it unto good, to bring to pass, as it is this day,

to save much people alive. Now therefore fear ye not: I will nourish you, and your little ones. And he comforted them, and spake kindly unto them. (Genesis 50:19-21)

Nowhere in the narrative of Joseph's life do we find him murmuring and complaining about his situation; neither is he found carrying a chip on his shoulders and blaming the whole world for his plight. There is no indication in the narrative of a mind, a move, or a motion for vengeance; and there is no mention of Joseph having a big pay-back plan for his brothers. Most of all, he didn't use his position of power and authority to punish his brothers for something that transpired many years prior. There is no doubt that Joseph's attitude and gift catapulted him into his destiny.

Here are some events that were strategic in Joseph's transition from prisoner to governor of Egypt.

1. *Joseph faced his tests with dignity.* Running from a test means running from destiny. When Joseph was sold to the Ishmaelite traders, it is not indicated in the narrative that he attempted to escape. He did not draft a plan to break out of Egypt. Although he was innocent, he remained in Egypt. Remaining in Egypt was ultimately beneficial for both Joseph and the entire tribe of Israel. This, in fact, tells us that the very thing we aspire from which to run away is the very thing that God wants to use in our transition and to get glory out of our lives. Joseph's attitude about his quandary was to stay put, humble himself, and "go through."

2. *Joseph did not bring suffering upon himself by making selfish and unwise choices.* Self-imposed suffering brings no glory to God. God gave Joseph favor after he arrived at Potiphar's house

and blessed everything he touched. He was elevated and made ruler of all of Potiphar's household and everything he owned. Blessings came to Potiphar's house because of Joseph.

⁵And it came to pass from the time that he had made him overseer in his house, and over all that he had, that the LORD blessed the Egyptian's house for Joseph's sake; and the blessing of the LORD was upon all that he had in the house and in the field. ⁶And he left all that he had in Joseph's hand; and he knew not ought he had, save the bread which he did eat. And Joseph was a goodly person, and well favoured. (Genesis 39:5-6)

Joseph passed the test on the first level by humbling himself. This was the BIG one. Joseph was a very handsome man according to scripture (Genesis 39:6). Potiphar's wife had her eyes on him and approached him to have sex with her. Joseph was a man of integrity and he had an unblemished character. I'm sure that, like most men, he had desires for the opposite sex. He could very easily have slept with Potiphar's wife, but he told her that her husband trusted him, and that he would not do such a thing and sin against God.

In response to the temptation, Joseph mentioned **two** things concerning two people. The two people Joseph mentioned were Potiphar (his earthly master) and God (his heavenly Master). To the two people that he mentioned, he showed accountability, unfeigned love, respect, loyalty, and unselfishness. If Joseph had only thought of himself and his "manly needs," he would probably have succumbed to the temptation; however, he refused to let his emotions and his zipper rule, run, or ruin his destiny. Imprisonment for lying with the king's wife is quite different from imprisonment for a false accusation of rape by the king's wife. It is possible that one of the reasons we do not pass some of our tests is because we show accountability only to ourselves and to no one else.

3. *Joseph did not abort the transition.* Joseph did not try to escape or prove his innocence when he was thrown in prison for a crime he did not commit. If he had escaped from prison, he would have missed God and the transition would have been aborted because it was in prison that he became known for interpreting dreams. He was in prison when he was summoned to go before Pharaoh. It was after he interpreted Pharaoh's dreams that he was elevated to governor of Egypt. God used Joseph's gift while he was in prison to bring him out of prison and before the king.

A man's gift maketh room for him, and bringeth him before great men. (Proverbs 18:16)

When we are going through the fire, we must not jump out of it because God has His own set time to deliver us. Timing is everything to God. Emotions can rise when we are suffering; however, God wants to prove to us that He alone is God, He is all-powerful, and He wants to get the glory. We must not allow ourselves to be taken in by emotions when we are suffering. We must allow God to form and shape us; and we must allow Him to take us to the place of pain and suffering. We must arm ourselves to suffer as Jesus suffered. Only pressed grapes can bring wine. Wine is representative of the Spirit. But it is only when the grapes are pressed and crushed that the wine is produced.

[1] Forasmuch then as Christ hath suffered for us in the flesh, arm yourselves likewise with the same mind: for he that hath suffered in the flesh hath ceased from sin; [2] That he no longer should live the rest of his time in the flesh to the lusts of men, but to the will of God. (1Peter 4:1-2)

There is a cross for everyone as Jesus stated in Mark 8:34:

...Whosoever will come after me, let him deny himself, and take up his cross, and follow me."

Suffering is part of our spiritual growth and development, growth and development is part of the growing process, and the growing process takes us to the place of maturity and destiny.

God ordered Joseph's steps from the time he left Canaan to the very end. Even the false accusation made against him by Potiphar's wife worked for him. Federal incarceration was merely a stepping stone to the palace. Standing in Pharaoh's presence in the palace and interpreting his dreams was Joseph's beginning. Joseph's gift of interpreting dreams and his ability to instruct Pharaoh on how to handle his affairs during the famine impressed Pharaoh enough to put Joseph in charge of all of Egypt.

➤ **Power Point!** *God gets no glory out of self-imposed suffering.*

2

TRANSITIONING AND DREAMS/VISIONS

Joseph's transition began after he revealed his dreams to his father and brothers. The interpretation of the dream was that they would bow before him and that he would rule over them. These were prophetic dreams from God. The prophecy did not begin with Joseph, it began with Abraham. Joseph was a descendant of Abraham and God used Joseph to help fulfill His promise to Abraham, and Abraham was, in fact, a dreamer.

[17] That in blessing I will bless thee, and in multiplying I will multiply thy seed as the stars of the heaven, and as the sand which is upon the sea shore; and thy seed shall possess the gate of his enemies; [18] And in thy seed shall all the nations of the earth be blessed; because thou hast obeyed my voice. (Genesis 22:17-18)

Abraham was Joseph's great-grandfather. It was Joseph that God chose to deliver his people from famine and to assist in fulfilling His promise to Abraham. If Joseph had not been in position and accomplished his mission with complete success, his family would have perished during the famine; however, we know that what God has spoken will come to pass. *Someone* was going to be in position when famine struck the land to save Jacob and his family, and *that* person was Joseph. God sent Joseph ahead of the famine to preserve his family, thus aiding in fulfilling the promise He made to Abraham.

God ordained that dreams and visions play a significant role in the lives of His people as we will see in the life of Joseph. God used dreams and visions in the Bible for a number of reasons, including:

- To comfort and confirm
- To warn
- To give directions and instructions

Examination of some Biblical dreamers and their dreams will help in understanding the purpose for which God used them.

Comfort and Confirm

Joseph's Dream (New Testament)
Joseph was comforted after knowing that Mary was pregnant by the Holy Ghost. God revealed the truth to him in a dream.

¹and not willing to make her a publick example, was minded to put her away privily. ²⁰ But while he thought on these things, behold, the angel of the Lord appeared unto him in a dream, saying, Joseph, thou son of David, fear not to take unto thee Mary thy wife: for that which is conceived in her is of the Holy Ghost. (Matthew 1:19-20).

²⁴ Then Joseph being raised from sleep did as the angel of the Lord had bidden him, and took unto him his wife: ²⁵ And knew her not till she had brought forth her firstborn son: and he called his name JESUS. (Matthew 1:24-25)

Jacob's dream – Jacob revived after hearing that his son, Joseph was still alive. God used a vision to bring comfort and confirmation to Jacob concerning the covenant that He had made with his father and grandfather. God assured Jacob that He would be with him on his way to Egypt and He would bring him out again, and make of him a great nation.

²And God spake unto Israel in the visions of the night, and said, Jacob, Jacob. And he said, Here am I. ³ And he said, I am God, the God of thy father: fear not to go down into Egypt; for I will there make of thee a great nation: ⁴ I will go down with thee into Egypt; and I will also surely bring thee up again: and Joseph shall put his hand upon thine eyes. (Genesis 46:2-4)

Gideon and the Midianite dreamer

Even though Gideon was a man of low self-esteem, God chose him to deliver Israel out of the hands of the Midianites.

And he said unto him, Oh my Lord, wherewith shall I save Israel? behold, my family is poor in Manasseh, and I am the least in my father's house. (Judges 6:15)

And the angel of the Lord appeared unto him, and said unto him, The LORD is with thee, thou mighty man of valour. (Judges 6:12)

And the LORD looked upon him, and said, Go in thy might, and thou shalt save Israel from the hand of the Midianites: have not I sent thee? (Judges 6:14)

God confirmed His word to Gideon several times before Gideon was almost convinced that he had been chosen for the task. It wasn't until God allowed Gideon to hear a Midianite's dream that he was totally convinced of his task. God told Gideon to go down to the Midianites' camp. When Gideon arrived, he heard a Midianite describing a dream he had to one of his companions:

And when Gideon was come, behold, there was a man that told a dream unto his fellow, and said, Behold, I dreamed a dream, and, lo, a cake of barley bread tumbled into the host of Midian, and came unto a tent, and smote it that it fell, and overturned it, that the tent lay along. ¹⁴ And his fellow answered and said, This is nothing else save the sword of Gideon the son of Joash, a man of Israel: for into his hand hath God delivered Midian, and all the host. (Judges 7:13, 14)

Gideon returned to his camp with total and absolute assurance that everything God had said to him was true. I can image Gideon running back to his camp with excitement and telling the boys to strap 'em up and let's go get 'em.

Gideon worshiped God after hearing the Midianite's dream and the interpretation. The conclusion of the story is that Gideon and his army of three hundred men defeated the Midianites in battle.

Thus was Midian subdued before the children of Israel, so that they lifted up their heads no more. And the country was in quietness forty years in the days of Gideon. (Judges 8:28)

To Warn

Abimelech's Dream
In fear of his life, Abraham told King Abimelech that Sarah was his sister. When Abimelech began to claim Sarah as his own, God warned Abimelech in a dream that he would die if he touched Sarah.

³ But God came to Abimelech in a dream by night, and said to him, Behold, thou art but a dead man, for the woman which thou has taken; for she is a man's wife. ⁴ But Abimelech had not come near her: and he said, Lord, wilt thou slay also a righteous nation? ⁵ Said he not unto me, She is my sister? and she, even she herself said, He is my brother: in the integrity of my heart and innocency of my hands have I done this. ⁶ And God said unto him in a dream, Yea, I know that thou didst this in the integrity of thy heart; for I also withheld thee from sinning against me: therefore suffered I thee not to touch her. ⁷ Now, therefore restore the man his wife; for he is a prophet, and he shall pray for thee, and thou shall live: and if thou restore her not, know that thou shalt surely die, thou, and all that are thine. (Genesis 20:3-7)

Abimelech immediately apologized to God, declared his innocence, and confronted Abraham about the matter. In the meantime, God had shut up the womb of Abimelech's wife. (Genesis 20:17-18). Abraham admitted that he had not told the truth and why. Abimelech returned Sarah to Abraham, along with gifts and women servants. God then opened the womb of Abimelech's wife and his maidservants'.

Pharaoh's Dream

Pharaoh had two disturbing dreams which he could not interpret. He consulted with his magicians but neither could they interpret the dreams.

And it came to pass at the end of two full years, that Pharaoh dreamed: and, behold, he stood by the river ² And, behold, there came up out of the river seven well favoured kine and fatfleshed; and they fed in a meadow.

³ And, behold, seven other kine came up after them out of the river, ill favoured and leanfleshed; and stood by the other kine upon the brink of the river. ⁴ And the ill favoured and leanfleshed kine did eat up the seven well favoured and fat kine. So Pharaoh awoke. ⁵ And he slept and dreamed the second time: and, behold, seven ears of corn came up upon one stalk, rank and good. ⁶ And, behold, seven thin ears and blasted with the east wind sprung up after them. ⁷ And the seven thin ears devoured the seven rank and full ears. And Pharaoh awoke, and, behold, it was a dream. (Genesis 41:1-7)

Two years prior to Pharaoh's dreams, Joseph had interpreted dreams for the butler and the baker while they were in prison together. The butler remembered that Joseph interpreted his and the baker's dreams, and he told Pharaoh. Pharaoh sent for Joseph, who, at the time, was still in prison for the false accusations made against him by Potiphar's wife. Pharaoh repeated the dreams to Joseph. The interpretation of the dreams was that seven years of famine followed by seven years of plenty was coming upon the land. After interpreting the dreams, Joseph gave Pharaoh divine instructions on how to manage the famine. With his wisdom and knowledge, Pharaoh appointed Joseph governor over the land to manage the years of famine and the years of plenty. (*Genesis 41:25-46*).

The Wise men's Dream

In the beginning of Matthew 2, Herod instructed the wise men to return to him when they found the child, Jesus, so that he could worship the child. However, Herod had no intent to worship the child, but to kill him. God instructed the wise men not to return to Herod.

And being warned of God in a dream that they should not return to Herod, they departed into their own country another way. (Matthew 2:12)

The wise men adhered the warning in the dream and refused the king's order.

Instructions/directions

As children of God, we are in constant need of instructions and directions from God in order to be in total alliance with His will. He uses angels, His audible voice, dreams and vision, however God is God, and has the right to instruct us in whatever way pleases Him.

Jacob's dream/Laban's dream

After spending more than twenty years in Laban's company, God appeared to Jacob in a dream and instructed him to leave and go back to his native land.

[11] And the angel of God spake unto me in a dream, saying, Jacob: And I said, Here am I. [12] And he said, Lift up now thine eyes, and see, all the rams which leap upon the cattle are ringstraked, speckled, and grisled: for I have seen all that Laban doeth unto thee. [13] I am the God of Bethel, where thou anointedst the pillar, and where thou vowedst a vow unto me: now arise, get thee out from this land, and return unto the land of thy kindred. (Genesis 31:11-13)

Jacob called his wives together and shared with them what God had said to him in a dream. He packed his possessions, gathered his family, and moved out. At the time, Laban had left to sheer his sheep and had been gone for three days. When he returned and learned that Jacob had left, he became absolutely furious and set out to find Jacob. On his voyage, God spoke to him in a dream:

And God came to Laban the Syrian in a dream by night, and said unto him, Take heed that thou speak not to Jacob either good or bad. (Genesis 31:24).

When Laban found Jacob, he came as close as he could to threatening him. No matter what he did, God had set the stage and there would be no violence.

Some Bible scholars suggest that dreams and visions are only used in the Old Testament, and that God no longer uses them to communicate with man. It is apparent by scripture that Paul, Peter, Ananias, John, and Cornelius had dreams and visions. Their dreams and visions were after the establishment of the church, which puts dreams and visions in the Church era. This is to say that God still uses dreams and visions to reveal His will unto man. Men will always have dreams and visions. It is established in Joel 2:28 and Acts 2:17that in the last days "your old men shall dream dreams and your young men shall see visions."

The dream Cornelius has of Peter
There was a certain man in Caesarea called Cornelius, a centurion of the band called the Italian band, ² A devout man, and one that feared God with all his house, which gave much alms to the people, and prayed to God alway. ³ He saw in a vision evidently about the ninth hour of the day an angel of God coming in to him, and saying unto him, Cornelius. ⁴ And when he looked on him, he was afraid, and said, What is it, Lord? And he said unto him, Thy prayers and thine alms are come up for a memorial before God. ⁵ And now send men to Joppa, and call for one Simon, whose surname is Peter: ⁶ He lodgeth with one Simon a tanner, whose house is by the sea side: he shall tell thee what thou oughtest to do. (Acts 10:1-6)

God was directing Peter and Cornelius in visons almost simultaneously. Cornelius was going to have the experience of his life, and so was Peter. God prepared Peter for a visitation with Cornelius because up to that point, Peter had not reached out to the Gentiles with the gospel. God showed Peter that He is not a respecter of persons and that the blood that Jesus shed on the cross was for "the world." God instructed Cornelius to send for Peter and where to find him. What a miraculous experience when Peter and Cornelius made contact! It resulted in Peter preaching the gospel of Jesus Christ to Cornelius, at which time Cornelius and his entire household was filled with the Holy Ghost, and they were baptized in the name of Jesus. (Acts 10:44-48)

Ananias' Dream of Paul
10 And there was a certain disciple at Damascus, named Ananias; and to him said the Lord in a vision, Ananias. And he said, Behold, I am here, Lord. 11 And the Lord said unto him, Arise, and go into the street which is called Straight, and enquire in the house of Judas for one called Saul, of Tarsus: for, behold, he prayeth, 12 And hath seen in a vision a man named Ananias coming in, and putting his hand on him, that he might receive his sight. (Acts 9:10-12)

Saul developed a very bitter reputation in the Christian community. He had killed many Christian men and women. Ananias had heard of Saul and his murderous mission. Incidentally, it was Saul who held the coats of those who stoned Stephen to death (*Acts 7:58-59*). It was the Damascus Road experience that Jesus revealed himself to Saul, after which his life changed forever. God changed his name from Saul to Paul. God showed Ananias that Paul had seen him putting his hand on him in a vision so that Paul may receive his sight. In addition, God told Ananias that Paul was a chosen vessel unto him (Acts 9:15).

There are other scriptures in the Bible where God used dreams and visions to show His will to His people, to instruct, warn, and direct them. There are also other scriptures in the Bible where God even showed dreams and visions to people of heathen nations. Nebuchadnezzar, the Midianite, and Belshazzar are a few examples.

Prophecy

The Beginning of Joseph's Transition in Egypt
Joseph was a prophetic dreamer. God used dreams as a means of prophecy to Joseph concerning his destiny. He had no confirmation

from anyone that what he saw in his dreams came from God. Even though his father did not show signs of total agreement with Joseph's dream, he did not totally dismiss it, but pondered over it after he slightly rebuked him. When God speaks to us, we must be convinced that it is, in fact, God speaking. It is good to seek confirmation, but only if we use that confirmation to assist us. Gideon sought confirmations from God that God was really going to use him to deliver the Israelites out of the hands of the Midianites, however, Gideon was not totally convinced that he was going to be used of God until after he heard the Midianite's dream and interpretation. God wants us to trust Him enough that He can say something only once, and we believe Him and act on it.

When God speaks, it doesn't matter if we receive confirmation from someone else or not. Joseph never received confirmation from anyone that he was going to rule over his family, nevertheless, it happened. No matter who is or is not convinced, we must hold fast to what God has shown us and understand that once God has spoken, it goes into motion; maybe slowly, but surely.

We will examine how Joseph's dreams played out in his future position as governor of Egypt. First of all, Joseph was his father's favorite son. For this reason, Joseph's ten brothers were very jealous of him, hated him, and as a result, plotted to kill him. Jacob gave Joseph a coat of many colors. Such a distinctive coat was a symbol of honor. It was predetermined that Joseph held a prominent position in the clan. Reuben, the oldest son was disinherited because he slept with Bilhah, one of Jacob's concubines.

To confirm his rank as ruler, God showed Joseph, not once, but twice that his position as ruler of the clan was undeniable (Genesis 37:5-9). Some people may suggest that Joseph made a mistake by telling his dreams to his brothers. I strongly disagree. The reason I disagree is that in the end, Joseph's brothers did certainly confirm within themselves that from the beginning, Joseph was destined to be ruler, and the dream that he told them prior to their coming to Egypt was confirmation. There was no doubt in their minds that the thirteen years prior, Joseph was "**the one**." His brothers were witnesses that the thing was established before Joseph was actually made governor of Egypt. In small terms, they were witnesses that Joseph was a dreamer as well as an interpreter of dreams.

Let us examine each of Joseph's prophetic dreams.

Dream number 1:

⁵ And Joseph dreamed a dream, and he told it his brethren: and they hated him yet the more. ⁶ And he said unto them, Hear, I pray you, this dream which I have dreamed: ⁷ For, behold, we were binding sheaves in the field, and, lo, my sheaf arose, and also stood upright; and behold, your sheaves stood around about, and made obeisance to my sheaf. (Genesis 37:5-7)

Dream number 2:

⁹ And he dreamed yet another dream, and told it his brethren, and said, Behold, I have dreamed a dream more; and, behold, the sun and the moon and the eleven stars made obeisance to me. ¹⁰ And he told it to his father, and to his brethren: and his father rebuked him, and said unto him, What is this dream that thou hast dreamed? Shall I and thy mother and thy brethren indeed come to bow down ourselves to thee to the earth? (Genesis 37:9-10)

The first dream unmistakably pointed out that Joseph's brothers would be humbled before him. Apparently, they figured out the interpretation without Joseph's aid. There was no symbolic interpretation required. The meaning of the dream was simple and clear cut.

And his brethren said to him, "Shalt thou indeed reign over us? Or shalt thou indeed have dominion over us? And they hated him yet the more for his dreams, and for his words. (Genesis 37:8)

The second dream was unambiguous, even though Joseph incurred some rebuke from his father. Although Joseph's father favored him and clothed him with the robe of honor, it appears that his father was annoyed about the second dream. Even so, from all indications, Jacob contemplated that there was some merit and significance to his son's dream.

And his brethren envied him; but his father observed the saying. (Genesis 37:11)

Jacob interpreted the dream to mean that he, (Jacob) was the sun, Leah was the moon, and the eleven brothers were the stars. Rachel was dead at that time and Leah was left to care for her two sons. There are quite a number of symbols, types, and shadows in the revelation of Joseph's dreams.

The number **two** had special significance in Joseph's life and is worthy of attention.

❖ Joseph had <u>two</u> dreams
❖ He interpreted <u>two</u> dreams while in prison
❖ He interpreted Pharaoh's <u>two</u> dreams
❖ He and his brother were the only <u>two</u> children to which their mother, Rachel gave birth
❖ He was in prison for <u>two</u> years after interpreting the prisoners' dreams
❖ <u>Two</u> sons were born to him in Egypt
❖ He had <u>two</u> pit experiences (his brothers threw him in a pit, and in Egypt, he was put in prison, which was a type of pit)
❖ <u>Two</u> years into the seven years of plenty, his father came to Egypt
❖ Joseph was sold <u>two</u> times: once to the Midianite traders and once to Potiphar
❖ He was given two coats while in Egypt

Joseph experienced quite a number of doubles in his lifetime. He even knew what the number two represented in Pharaoh's two dreams. The only doubles that he had not experienced at the time of interpreting Pharaoh's dream was his two sons, who had not yet been born, and his father's arrival in Egypt during the second year of the famine.

And for that the dream was doubled unto Pharaoh twice; it is because the thing is established by God, and God will shortly bring it to pass. (Genesis 41:32)

In conclusion, Joseph was a prophetic dreamer. His dreams were fulfilled in Egypt. Prophecy from God isn't always fulfilled the same day, the next day, or even the next year. Joseph spent thirteen years in Egypt before he became governor of Egypt. He spent thirteen years preparing for his destiny.

Everything that occurred in Joseph's life subsequent to his dreams was connected to the fulfillment of his destiny, even the false accusation made against him by Potiphar's wife. The interpretation of the dreams was undoubtedly that Joseph's father, mother, and eleven brothers would one day come humbly before him. Although Jacob did not know the absolute gravity of Joseph's dreams, he knew there was substance to them. Joseph's transition began soon after the prophetic dreams.

Prophecy is prophecy, whether it comes in the form of a dream, an audible voice from God, one of God's prophets, or a vision. No matter when a dream occurs, if it is truly from God, just wait; it will surely come to pass.

> ➢ **Power Point!** *Dreams and visions have always been a means of communication between God and man.*

3

IT HAPPENED SUDDENLY

It is absolutely amazing the way in which life can change so dramatically in *just one day*! Joseph served time in federal prison because of a false accusation made against him by Potiphar's wife. All of a sudden, one day, he was being told to shave, change clothes, and come before the king.

"Then Pharaoh sent and called Joseph, and they brought him hastily out of the dungeon: and he shaved himself, and changed his raiment, and came in unto Pharaoh. (Genesis 41:14)

And in the same day, his life was totally changed. He wasn't given time to think about what had happened, to go back to his cell to get things organized, or time to say "goodbye" to his cellmates. In the matter of a day, Joseph was released, exonerated, and made governor. WOW! It was like transitioning from a state of homelessness to a mansion in Beverly Hills, all in the same day...sort of like the story of the Beverly Hillbillies. Joseph had a "suddenly" experience. God hastened His word to perform it in Joseph's life. What an awesome transition! No one can have such a phenomenal experience without the hand of God. How is it that a man is taken by force to a strange land, made a slave in that same land, go to prison, and become second in command in *that same land* on which he was made a slave? Only God can take such an unparalleled situation and make it work for the good of all those involved.

When a man's ways please the LORD, he maketh even his enemies to be at peace with him. (Proverbs 16:7).

In just one day:

- ❖ He was given a vesture of linen - a silk garment worn by the Egyptian priesthood. *(Genesis 41:42)*
- ❖ He was given a ring- with the king's name and seal; used for the purpose of doing business transactions. *(Genesis 41:42)*
- ❖ He was given a golden chain-symbolizing dignity and royalty; worn by rulers and those in high ranking positions. *(Genesis 41:42)*
- ❖ He was given a wife of high-ranking status-Joseph married Asenath, a woman whose family was very influential in Egypt, and from a priestly family. *(Genesis 41:45)*
- ❖ God flipped the script and made Joseph master over his master, Potiphar. *(Genesis 41:40)*
- ❖ His name was changed from Joseph to Zaphnathpaneah. *(Genesis 41:45)*
- ❖ Instead of having to bow to others, others were ordered to bow to Joseph. *(Genesis 41:43)*
- ❖ He was given the second chariot to Pharaoh. *(Genesis 41:43)*

Before Joseph stepped into his destiny, he endured:

- rejection from his brothers
- isolation from his family
- lies
- a false accusation
- shame
- embarrassment

- imprisonment without provocation
- the absence of his father in his life
- possible emotional trauma due to the absence of his father in his life.

For thirteen years he lived the life of a slave; for thirteen years, no doubt, he yearned for his father's presence, affection, love and emotional support; and for thirteen years, he lived in a foreign country and had to become accustomed to a culture with which he was forced to become familiar.

➤ **Power Point!** *It is absolutely amazing the way in which life can change so dramatically in just one day.*

4

OVERCOMING TEMPTATION
IN TRANSITION

Having an affair was not part of Joseph's dreams. Who can imagine what would have happened to Joseph if he had allowed Potiphar's wife to seduce him? He would have lost his integrity and his good name, and Potiphar probably would have had his head taken off. We must be very careful that we do not let the enemy slip things into our lives that are not part of our dreams and our destinies. Elements that we allow to come into our lives that are not part of our dreams can cause momentous setbacks and grave delays.

Unlike Joseph, many men have been brought to low esteem because they failed to control their zipper. An overwhelming number of men have lost their ministries, jobs, wives, and entire families due to their inability to control their sex drive. Others have opened doors in their lives that have caused generational curses. Some have ushered in trans-generational issues upon themselves and their children.

King David's fall with Bathsheba is a typical example of what can happen when the zipper is not contained. Bathsheba became pregnant when she and David committed adultery. David tried to cover his sin by having Bathsheba's husband killed. Several things happened as a result of their action.

1. **A spirit of perversion nested in David's family.**

Amnon, David's son raped his own sister, Tamar.

[10] And Amnon said unto Tamar, Bring the meat into the chamber, that I may eat of thine hand. And Tamar took the cakes which she had made, and brought them into the chamber to Amnon her brother. [11] And when she had brought them unto him to eat, he took hold of her, and said unto her, Come lie with me, my sister. [12] And she answered him, Nay, my brother, do not force me; for no such thing ought to be done in Israel: do not thou this folly. [13] And I, whither shall I cause my shame to go? and as for thee, thou shalt be as one of the fools in Israel. Now therefore, I pray thee, speak unto the king; for he will not withhold me from thee. [14] Howbeit he would not hearken unto her voice: but, being stronger than she, forced her, and lay with her. (2 Samuel 13:10-14)

David's concubines was raped by his son, Absalom

Thus said the LORD, Behold, I will raise up evil against thee out of thine own house, and I will take thy wives before thine eyes, and give them unto thy neighbor, and he shall lie with thy wives in the sight of this sun. (2 Samuel 12:11)

So they spread Absalom a tent upon the top of the house; and Absalom went in unto his father's concubines in the sight of all of Israel. (2 Samuel 16:22)

2. **A curse of war and violence entered David's family.**

God told David through the prophet, Nathan, that the sword would never leave his house because he took a man's wife.

Now therefore the sword shall never depart from thine house; because thou hast despised me, and hast taken the wife of Uriah the Hittite to be thy wife. (2 Samuel 12:10)

Absalom murdered Amnon, his brother, because Amnon raped their sister, Tamar.

And Absalom spake unto his brother Amnon neither good nor bad: for Absalom hated Amnon, because he had forced his sister Tamar. (2 Samuel 13:22)
²⁸ Now Absalom had commanded his servants, saying, Mark ye now when Amnon's heart is merry with wine, and when I say unto you, Smite Amnon; then kill him, fear not: have not I commanded you? be courageous, and be valiant. ²⁹ And the servants of Absalom did unto Amnon as Absalom had commanded. Then all the king's sons arose, and every man gat him up upon his mule, and fled. (2 Samuel 13:28, 29)

Absalom was killed while revolting against his father, King David.

¹⁴ ...And he took three darts in his hand, and thrust them through the heart of Absalom, while he was yet alive in the midst of the oak. ¹⁵ And ten young men that bare Joab's armour compassed about and smote Absalom, and slew him. (2 Samuel 18:14-15)

¹⁷ And they took Absalom, and cast him into a great pit in the wood, and laid a very great heap of stones upon him: and all Israel fled everyone to his tent. (2 Samuel 18:17)

After David's fall with Bathsheba, violence and sexual perversion nested in his family because he had Bathsheba's husband killed, which was orchestrated because of his erotic, sexual behavior. His life was not what it could have been had he contained himself. God told David that he would have given him anything he asked. But because he murdered a man and took his wife, he brought a curse upon his house. He had an innocent man killed, and this caused the death of his firstborn son by Bathsheba. What a horrible price to pay for a few minutes of sexual pleasure! These statements are in no way meant to demean David, but to prove a point of what happens when we let temptation overtake us and we move in our flesh.

Howbeit, because by this deed thou hast given great occasion to the enemies of the LORD to blaspheme, the child also that is born unto thee shall surely die. (2 Samuel 12:14)

Some people feel that they cannot relate to Jesus' ability to control Himself because He was God manifested in the flesh. Some people feel that Jesus had more power than we have to contain ourselves; however, the Bible says that He was also tempted but did not sin.

For we have not an high priest which cannot be touched with the feeling of our infirmities; but was in all points tempted like as we are, yet without sin. (Hebrews 4:15)

This means that Jesus dealt with the same human elements such as pain and emotions that we possess, yet He was without sin. If we cannot relate to Jesus, then, we can relate to Joseph. Joseph had a great opportunity to have sexual relations with Potiphar's wife. She consistently pursued Joseph. How many men have blamed women when committing adultery with her, claiming he was seduced and pursued? Well, consider Joseph! Potiphar's wife tried to seduce Joseph, but he fled from her. Why? Because he loved God, was loyal to his master, and refused to let his zipper rule.

Some men feel a sense of power and control over another man when he can sleep with his wife. Joseph did not have such an attitude. He knew who he was, and he was secure in his position in Potiphar's house. He humbled himself to the situation at hand until God elevated him.

Men and women alike can learn a very valuable lesson by considering what happened with David as opposed to what happened with Joseph when they were tempted. Men, women, and children are suffering unnecessarily because one man or one woman refused to keep their sex drive in check. Many people have been destroyed, pastors have had to give up their congregations, sheep have been scattered, children have been raised without their fathers and mothers, and other innocent people have suffered emotionally because someone thought that sexual pleasure was more important. Thank God for a Joseph example.

> ➢ **Power Point!** *Elements that we allow to come into our lives that are not part of our dreams can cause momentous setbacks and grave delays.*

5

JOSEPH'S OUTSTANDING CHRIST-LIKE TRAITS

Joseph had an impeachable character and a flawless record of faithfulness. When confronted by Potiphar's wife, he exemplified and maintained a true sense of moral purity. Joseph proved to be trust worthy and he remained pure during temptation. Joseph was not God manifested in flesh, as Jesus was; however, in his experiences, he exhibited Christ-like traits such as no other character in Bible history. His life is more blameless than any other Bible character. Let us examine a few of these Christ-like traits.

A. Forgave His Enemies

It takes a *real* man to forgive. Anyone can hold a grudge. Anyone can show off their position of power and authority over other individuals in a time of crisis, but a *real* man will humble himself and let the power of God luster. Joseph exemplified the true nature of Christ. He clearly demonstrated the love and compassion that Jesus displayed toward those in need. Ultimately, Joseph illustrated the spirit of forgiveness like no other character in Bible history, besides Stephen.

Now therefore fear ye not: I will nourish you, and your little ones. And he comforted them, and spake kindly unto them. (Genesis 50:21).

What love and compassion Joseph displayed toward his brothers! What a powerful demonstration of humility! What a powerful, yet humbling position to hold! Jesus could not have been more pleased with Joseph's response in his situation. To prove that God was exceptionally pleased with Joseph's attitude toward his brothers and the way in which Joseph handled the situation, He made Joseph's enemies be at peace with him in the most acquiescent way.

When a man's ways please the LORD, he maketh even his enemies to be at peace with him. (Proverbs 16:7).

God prepared a table before Joseph in the presence of his enemies (Psalms 23:5). Clearly, the Word of God was vigorous in Joseph's life. To take it a step further, twice in Genesis 50, after their father died, Joseph had to calm his brothers' fears and reassure them that he would not retaliate. He was in a position where he could either calm their fears or make them feel very nervous and intimidated. Joseph, with a heart like the Christ that he had not met in person, responded with the former attitude. It is my estimation that Joseph's willingness to forgive his brothers is what caused him to rise to the next highest level of authority in Egypt. (Genesis 50:19; 21)

If we do not forgive one another, God will not forgive us.

[15] But if ye forgive not men their trespasses, neither will your Father forgive your trespasses (Matthew 6:15).

God would have not elevated Joseph to such a position if he had allowed an unforgiving spirit to linger in his heart against his brothers. Over a thirteen year period, Joseph had time to decide if he would live a life of bondage by not forgiving his brothers or if he would live a life of freedom by forgiving. God has instructed us to forgive and it is quite clear what happens if we refuse. Joseph exemplified forgiveness in such a way that it has intimately touched the very hearts of those who have heard or read about his humble and notable acts toward his brothers.

B. Shared success with those who hated him

Joseph had no problem sending for his entire family after he revealed his identity to his brothers. There was no reservation or hesitation on his part to share his wealth and riches. How many of us can truly say that we are willing to forgive our enemies and share our wealth with them? Jesus Christ died for our salvation, but He also died that we may live in health and wealth, even after we crucified Him.

Beloved, I wish above all things that thou mayest prosper and be in health, even as thy soul prospereth. (III John 2)

C. Did not run away from destiny

Do we really want to go where God wants to take us? It isn't always easy to say "yes" to God, especially when we feel that our suffering is without provocation. Pain, tests, and trials are strategically designed for each of us, and if we do not go through successfully, we will repeat the process, which will only prolong our destinies.

One of the things that I love about Joseph is that he did not attempt to break out of prison to get back home to daddy. He held on to his integrity and did not blame the world for his dilemma. He humbled himself and bore his cross; and unless we humble ourselves, we will never be what God has destined and designed us to be. God designs our trials and tests, and consequently, our lives are shaped into what He desires. We will only reflect Jesus if we humble ourselves as He did.

> ➤ ***Power Point!*** *Anyone can show off their position of power and authority over other individuals in a time of crisis, but a real man will humble himself and let the power of God luster.*

6

ELEMENTS OF THE STRANGE PLACE

There are common elements that reside in a place with which we are unfamiliar; this is especially true in the Christian/ Church/Body of Christ arena. When our lives are orchestrated by God, there are certain elements that we encounter with which we are not always comfortable. For instance, adjusting to a new congregation is not always a comfortable change. Listed below are some elements of change during transition.

> ➢ *A new Congregation:* God sends us into various areas of the vineyard to work, and as we do so, we may encounter people in ministry who are innately territorial about accepting certain people into their ministry. Their actions may cause conflict and even bring on spiritual warfare. All of God's people are not very nice or kind in the reception area. The enemy does not want us to live inside of God's will. He is an adversary of our unity and obedience to God. No matter what occurs, as long as we know that we are in God's will, we are safe, and God will intervene on our behalf.
>
> My advice to any person that may be experiencing conflict with someone who is territorial is to stay with the ministry regardless of the attitude of the leader of the ministry. There

will come a time that God will intervene and He will surely give instructions and bring a resolution. God will hold us totally responsible for being in His will; and it doesn't matter who opposes our presence. God will deal with leaders of ministries in His own time and in His own way. We need only to stand still and watch God work on our behalf.

> *A New Ministry:* As we follow God, we will give birth to new ministries. We must not allow fear to grip our hearts if we are going to step out and do what God has commanded. A new ministry may take us inside correctional institutions. It may take us to larger congregations or multitudes. If we are accustomed and comfortable with only ministering to small crowds, ministering to multitudes of thousands would be quite an adjustment and a challenge as well. God may even lead us to unsaved loved ones with whom we may have unresolved issues. Lastly, God may lead us to other countries to spread the gospel. No matter what the gift, calling, or anointing, we must know that God is in control. Fear of the strange place will subside when we learn to trust God.

> *A New Leader:* When encountering a new congregation, there is also a new pastor. Well, sometimes, pastors may not know where we have been or where we are going and may need to get familiar with us. This may not be easy for some of them because of the unfamiliarity. God tells us to know those who labor among us. Knowing those who labor among us may take some time. Some new pastors that we encounter may have trust issues and need God to show and teach them how to deal with new members. Some new pastors, on the other hand, have built barriers for other apparent or unapparent reasons. Some pastors have seen so many people come and go in their congregations until they have conditioned themselves not to trust those who

have not been a part of the ministry for some time. And some pastors have become numb to those who enter. Other pastors may want a newcomer of a congregation to sit for years before they work in any ministry of the congregation, or in their calling; however, even the pastor must know what God has to say about it. Some pastors demand new members (no matter how long they have been a Christian or no matter where they are in Christ) to attend many classes, such as a new members and foundation class before working in their ministry or moving about in the congregation. Some new members are ready to begin working for Christ and do not require years of sitting before being used; however, some members may be just as hesitant to work as the pastor is to allow them to work in the ministry. But it's okay. God will bring to pass His purpose for placing us wherever we are placed. In all our ways, we are to acknowledge God and He tells us that He will direct our path. God knows when an individual is really ready to move in or out. God will work His will no matter what; where He leads us, He will keep us.

➤ *A New Gift:* God could possibly unveil a gift in us that was not known. Exercising a newly discovered gift may be uncomfortable at the beginning. We must not shy away from a new gift but embrace it because in the end, it will be used to glorify God and bring comfort, exhortation, and edification to the body of Christ.

➤ *New Acquaintances:* When we enter new territory, a new congregation, a different part of God's vineyard, or a new ministry, we also encounter people that we have never met. No matter where we go, people are the same. Christians can sometimes be the hardest people with which to connect, make friends, or work with at times. The Holy Spirit is one Spirit with one mission; however, people are comprised of different emotions, attitudes, thoughts, ideas, and concepts. Elements of human nature can sometimes make things difficult as we try and work together in ministry. When we are not in the spirit, our human emotions can sometimes surface in a very bad way, causing conflict and pain to those in close proximity. We must guard our hearts and make sure that we do not allow other people to change our atmosphere, cause us to succumb to their issues, or change our character. And as ministry leaders, we must make sure that we are not causing undue conflict and pain to those around us.

➤ **Power Point!** God will work His will no matter what; where He leads us, He will keep us.

7

SURVIVING THE UNFAMILIAR PLACE

We must allow God to take us to the unfamiliar place. An unfamiliar place can be any test, trial, or territory that we've never treaded. It can also be a familiar place but strange or unfamiliar surroundings. It can be any situation or circumstance that is new to us.

Joseph experienced at least eight strange or unfamiliar elements in Egypt:

❖ People
❖ Environment
❖ Atmosphere
❖ Culture
❖ Language
❖ Slavery
❖ Prison

Every area that Joseph encountered was unfamiliar, and to say the least, uncomfortable; however, Joseph humbled himself to the unfamiliar place with a very positive attitude. Humility, along with a positive attitude helped to catapult him into his destiny without getting distracted or stuck in the process. Fighting, kicking, screaming, murmuring, complaining, grumbling, and rebelling against the process only makes it longer and more difficult. An example of this happened with the children of Israel:

[27] How long shall I bear with this evil congregation, which murmur against me? I have heard the murmurings of the children of Israel, which they murmur against me.

[28] Say unto them, As truly as I live, saith the Lord, as ye have spoken in mine ears, so will I do to you:

[29] Your carcases shall fall in this wilderness; and all that were numbered of you, according to your whole number, from twenty years old and upward which have murmured against me. (Numbers 14:27-29)

Moses sent twelve men (one man from each tribe) to spy out the land of Canaan. Out of twelve men, only two came back with a positive report. It is absolutely amazing how that could have actually happened. All of the spies saw the exact same thing with their physical eyes; however, their perceptions divided when their eyes made contact with their spirit. It is also amazing how those ten men were so influential in their report that they were able to convince the entire camp that it was impossible for them to go over into Canaan. Joshua and Caleb were the only two of the twelve spies to give a positive report.

[32] But as for you, your carcases, they shall fall in this wilderness. [33] And your children shall wander in the wilderness forty years, and bear your whoredoms, until your carcases be wasted in the wilderness. [34] After the number of the days in which ye searched the land, even forty days, each day for a year, shall ye bear your iniquities, even forty years, and ye shall know my breach of promise. (Numbers 14:32-34)

Again, we must allow God to take us to uncomfortable zones without reservations. Being uncomfortable for merely a moment in time is well worth the goodies in the end. It never feels good to go from being comfortable to being uncomfortable, from feeling safe to dropping our safety net and following God. God is in control and if we remain in the race, we will make it to the finish line with success.

Babies cry when they enter the world for the first time. They do not cry because they are hungry, that their diapers need changing, or that they have been hurt in any manner. They cry simply because their comfort has been disturbed. For nine months they were fed perfunctorily, surrounded by warmth, and not having to breathe on their own. Then, suddenly, they are outside of their mother's womb and breathing independently. They are in a totally new environment, their umbilical cord has been cut, and they are operating somewhat independently of Mom. Crying is their way of saying, "send me back from whence I came; I do not want to be here; you've taken me out of my comfort zone." The crying continues until the infant is pacified. Crying is not an indication that the spirit needs to be soothed, but the flesh. The infant eventually adjusts to the environment after being out of the womb for a while, and the crying subsides. Some Christians tend to perform like babies. Sometimes we whine, kick, cry, and fight while going through transition.

God is definitely concerned with the pain, hurt, wounds, and discomfort we experience as we journey to the unfamiliar place; however, He wants us to grow up to be strong, healthy, vibrant Christians. He eventually wants to see the reflection of His Son, Jesus Christ in us. Therefore, crying, pouting, kicking, whining, murmuring and complaining will not cause God to change His mind enough to take us out of the unfamiliar place. We must take the good with the bad, the bitter with the sweet, the mountains with the valleys, and the joy with the sorrow if we are to be what God has destined us to be. And we know that all of these things will work for our good because we love God and we are called according to His purpose. *(Romans 8:28)*

➢ **Power Point!** *Being uncomfortable for merely a moment in time is well worth the goodies in the end.*

8

LETTING GO OF THE OLD AND EMBRACING THE NEW/IMPULSES OF TRANSITION

Letting go of the old and embracing the new can be very difficult sometimes because it demands "change." Change can be very intimidating. It is a place where one thing has ended and another is about to begin. It is the place of uncertainty. Uncertainty lies between the door that just closed and the door that is not quite opened. The space in-between the two doors can sometimes feel like a place of isolation, emptiness, and loneliness. It is the waiting room. Patience is a necessity, and endurance is a must.

We become vulnerable and fragile to God when we are going through major transitions because it becomes the time when we must trust Him in a very unique way-stepping out on nothing and believing that something is there. Though it is a fragile place and a fragile time, it is a very favorable place and time for God, however, because it is a time when God can show us who He is and what He can do; a time when He can flex His spiritual muscles and use us as trophies to show the world just how powerful He **really** is.

Beginning a new phase or experience in life can be just as dramatic as leaving an old one. The children of Israel became disoriented from time to time when they were transitioning from Egypt to the Promised Land. They were experiencing a new phase in their lives and an altogether new environment. They even had a new name, "children of Israel." They had a problem giving up the onions, leeks, garlic, and melons and all the foods that they had become comfortable eating in Egypt. God wanted to show them a new way. He fed them His food, manna, from heaven. They had to embrace a new eating habit and different food, which they considered hard to do because they had to depend solely on God for it. God knew that they were experiencing something new, and He was always ready to show Himself strong and mighty. He became their Jehovah-jireh.

Even though David had been anointed king of Israel, he waited on his time to take the throne. During David's time of transition, he experienced extreme trauma from King Saul. Many times he had to run for his life. Although David had opportunities to kill King Saul and take his place as king, he refused to touch God's anointed. He went through his tests and trials with King Saul until King Saul and his sons were killed in battle. When David's days of running from King Saul were finally over, he could rejoice because he made humble choices to spare King Saul's life more than once. That was the heart of God!

Some transitions are rapid while others are gradual. Sometimes God will interrupt our lives abruptly and cause us to immediately transition. Such a rate of transition can sometimes be very stimulating as well as extremely testing. Clinging tenaciously to the past only prolongs the inevitable. Giving up the old is a necessary condition for embracing the new. Holding on to the past does not make the pain of transition easier. Even if the transition is coming on abruptly, we must remember that we are not in it alone, and that we will come through successfully because God ordained it.

Trying to end a transition period before time can be absolutely devastating. It may cause a setback. We must remember that God ordered the transition and whatever He begins, He will end on time. We must exercise patience, endurance, longsuffering, and trust in God in order to have a successful transition. Moving ahead of God only leads to failure.

Certain impulses can accompany transition. The first impulse is **the feeling that we do not have control anymore**. This is especially true because God is taking us to another place and in order to get where He is taking us, we must surrender our total will and tell God, *"thy will be done."*

The second impulse is what I call the **"air walk."** An air walk is the feeling that we have when we are totally trusting God. We may even feel sometimes that God is not there at all. It is similar to Jesus' expression when He was hanging on the cross. He was hanging between heaven and earth...literally. He made the statement..."my God, my God, why hast thou forsaken me?" (Matthew 27:46) Even though we feel that nothing is holding us up, we already know what the outcome is going to be; however, we must remember that God has already assured us that we triumph in Christ...that means in transition also. Jesus' outcome was that He was resurrected just as He had told His disciples. Walking on air can be the same as God taking away our security blanket and leaving us to hold on to God for absolute and sheer comfort.

The third impulse of transition is **menopause** (men/o/pause). During menopause, life can be interrupted with headaches, hot flashes, mood swings, loss of weight, and other physical and emotional experiences. During transition, we may experience many changes. The old term for menopause is "the change of life." Transitioning from one stage or phase of our spiritual journey to another brings about changes in which our entire spirituality experiences major adjustments. Sometimes God takes us to a part of the vineyard that produces challenges that we have never experienced. Sometimes He simply takes us from one physical place to another...which automatically elicits transition. He may even take us to a place that will change our outlook on some old thoughts, behaviors, and beliefs. This is especially true when we are leaving a world of religious principles and embracing kingdom principles.

The fourth impulse of transition can be **reluctance**. Giving in to this impulse will only add considerable pain and discomfort to our lives as we transition. In order to reach the plateau designed for our lives, we must not be reluctant to go through transition. When I was transitioning from Ohio to Illinois, there was territory that I had to tread that I said I would never tread. The very territory that I said I would not tread became the very territory that I absolutely *had* to tread in order to experience what God had for me, and for my next level. At first I was reluctant to go, and I developed a negative attitude. The attitude dissipated when I finally came to the conclusion that humility, submission, contentment, and acceptance were necessary elements of my experience. It was not very long before I dropped the attitude and learned a very valuable lesson that enabled me to go through my transition easier. I even completed two Master Degrees during the process.

> ➤ **Power Point!** *Clinging tenaciously to the past only prolongs the inevitable. Giving up the old is a necessary component for embracing the new.*

9

THE POSITIVE AND POWERFUL USE OF ENEMIES IN TRANSITION

Joseph's father loved him very much and favored him above his other brothers, and for that reason, they hated him. After unveiling two dreams to his family that he would rule over them, his brothers hated him even more. The perfect opportunity presented itself one day and his brothers plotted to kill him.

And when they saw him afar off, even before he came near unto them, they conspired against him to slay him. (Genesis 37:18)

Joseph's brothers did not know, however, that God was in the plan. They were used as tools in Joseph's transition.

Joseph's brothers became his enemies and were used in God's divine plan for Joseph to reach his destiny. It was Jesus' enemies also that said, "Crucify him" (Mark 15:13). We will never reach our destinies without enemies. Both Jesus and Joseph triumphed over their enemies.

We do not always see the need to have certain people in our lives or in our circles because they will challenge us or bring us to our knees. We want them out of our ministries and out of our lives. God said that He would make our enemies our foot stool, which indicates that enemies would be there. He even said that if our ways please Him, He would make our enemies be at peace with us. He did not say that the enemy would not play a role. Jesus was God manifested in the flesh, yet, He did not tell Judas to go away. He announced that one in the group would betray Him. He simply allowed Judas to remain in the ministry and in his position as treasurer. Many pastors and leaders probably would have rebuked Judas in front of the entire church, dismissed him from the ministry, possibly put him out of the congregation, and thought they were doing God's will.

Jesus did not send Judas on his way, and he did not team up with the other disciples against Judas, although Judas **did** have evil in his heart. (Luke 22:3). Jesus did what some pastors and leaders can learn to do at times when the enemy gets busy in the ministry--simply **allow Judas to hang himself**. Judas could only go so far in his betrayal because money only takes us so far. Mammon has an end just as it has a beginning. Judas was used to catapult Jesus into his destiny. If the enemy would not have been used in such a way, the plan would not have been successful. The plan was successful because Judas played his part. Members of the Sanhedrin court needed a vessel through which to make their plan succeed. Judas was that vessel. Jesus understood that without enemies, He would not have reached His destiny. Everything that happens in our lives, if our steps are ordered by God, will catapult us into our destiny.

Enemies can be useful in our lives because they:

- Cause us to pray more
- Help to keep us on our feet, and alert
- Help to keep us close to God
- Help to keep us seeking God
- Help to keep us humble
- Chase us back to God when we stray

➢ **Power Point!** *Everything that happens in our lives, if our steps are ordered by God, will help catapult us into our destinies.*

10

THE SIMEON EFFECT IN JOSEPH'S LIFE

Simeon was very influential within the tribe. He exhibited an abysmal character and he used his destructive influence to do mischief, harm, and create discord. Simeon and Levi caused near irreversible damage to the clan on two distinct occasions.

1. The first occasion was concerning Dinah, the only female in the clan. Dinah was sexually assaulted by Shechem, a Canaanite prince. After the attack, Shechem's father, Hamor, asked Jacob if he would give Dinah to his son in marriage. The marriage was agreed to under the condition that the townsmen become circumcised (Genesis 34:14-16). The covenant was established and the circumcision was put in motion. On the day of circumcision when the men were most sore, Simeon and Levi executed a massacre on the camp of Shechem. They killed Shechem, Hamor, and all the men. They took the wives and children captive and retrieved the wealth of the land (Genesis 34:25-30). It may appear that the punishment far outweighed the crime. Jacob rebuked Simeon and Levi for the massacre. When Jacob was on his dying bed in Egypt, he called all of his sons to his bedside and told them their future. This was Simeon's lot:

⁵ Simeon and Levi are brethren; instruments of cruelty are in their habitations. ⁶ O my soul, come not thou into their secret; unto their assembly, mine honour, be not thou united: for in their anger they slew a man, and in their selfwill they digged down a wall. ⁷ Cursed be their anger, for it was fierce; and their wrath, for it was cruel: I will divide them in Jacob, and scatter them in Israel. (Genesis 49:5-7)

2. The second occasion is when Joseph was sent to check on his brothers in Shechem. It is suggested by scholars that Simeon led the assault against Joseph. Reuben suggested they throw Joseph down an empty well. Judah suggested they sell him. His brothers threw him in a pit. Simeon was used to help pilot Joseph to his destiny. Simeon rewarded himself with a pit experience in Egypt. When the same ten brothers went to Egypt to buy grain during the famine, Joseph accused them of being spies. They were demanded to leave and return with their younger brother after telling Joseph about him. Joseph held Simeon as surety for their return of Benjamin.

And he turned himself about from them, and wept; and returned to them again, and communed with them, and took from them Simeon, and bound him before their eyes. (Genesis 42:24)

And he said, Peace be to you, fear not: your God, and the God of your father, hath given you treasure in your sacks: I had your money. And he brought Simeon out unto them. (Genesis 43:23)

Presumably, Joseph knew of Simeon's character as a troublemaker, so he held him at bay to make sure he would not influence the others. Simeon's destructive leadership in such a delicate situation and at such a fragile time would not have been profitable. Joseph could not take a chance on Simeon affecting the group at a time when he wanted so desperately to see his little brother, Benjamin, and to know about his father's wellbeing. Simeon, presumably the instigator of the plot to destroy Joseph, was only an instrument to pilot Joseph to his destiny. Joseph's destiny was to deliver his people from famine.

> **Power Point!** *Simeon was only an instrument to pilot Joseph into his destiny.*

11

DIVINE PURPOSE AND DESTINY

We are all born with a divine purpose which was determined by God before we were conceived. God was not caught off-guard when we were born. Destiny and purpose met us here. In fact, before mom and dad came together in union, God knew us:

Before I formed thee in the belly, I knew thee; and before thou camest out of the womb I sanctified thee... (Jeremiah 1:5)

God had declared Joseph's beginning from his end before Joseph began his journey. When he was sold into Egypt, it appeared as if Joseph's life would end in total disaster, especially after his encounter with Potiphar's wife. But Egypt was just the beginning of an end that had already been declared. The events in Joseph's life prior to becoming governor could in no wise dictate or control what would be his destiny. What Joseph experienced in the beginning of his journey was only part of the true outcome. The end of what was to be was already declared and established while he was yet in his mother's womb. Joseph was destined to be victorious and defeat was not in the script.

Although some Bible characters may not have necessarily known their purpose before they reached their destiny, they all had a divine purpose. Sometimes, it takes years before we know the true purpose for which God has specifically ordained us. For instance:

Samson

Samson's purpose was to save Israel from the hands of the Philistines.

For, lo, thou shalt conceive, and bear a son; and no razor shall come on his head: for the child shall be a Nazarite unto God from the womb: and he shall begin to deliver Israel out of the hand of the Philistines. (Judges 13:5)

Samson had a weakness for ungodly women who did not love him. He was a man of God who had a problem containing his zipper and ended up in bed with a very seductive woman who betrayed and deceived him:

⁴ And it came to pass afterward, that he loved a woman in the valley of Sorek, whose name was Delilah. ⁵ And the lords of the Philistines came up unto her, and said unto her, Entice him, and see wherein his great strength lieth, and by what means we may prevail against him, that we may bind him to afflict him; and we will give thee every one of us eleven hundred pieces of silver. (Judges 16:4, 5)

¹⁸ And when Delilah saw that he had told her all his heart, she sent and called for the lords of the Philistines, saying, Come up this once, for he hath shewed me all his heart. Then the lords of the Philistines came up unto her, and brought money in their hand. (Judges 16:18)

²¹ But the Philistines took him, and put out his eyes, and brought him down to Gaza, and bound him with fetters of brass; and he did grind in the prison house. (Judges 16: 21)

Samson's parents warned him not to pursue women of the world; however, God used this situation to deliver Israel from the hand of the Philistines. Samson killed more Philistines in his death than he did during his lifetime. Samson's purpose was to deliver Israel from the hands of the Philistines; God said that he would deliver Israel, and that is exactly what happened, even in Samson's disobedience.

³⁰ And Samson said, Let me die with the Philistines. And he bowed himself with all his might; and the house fell upon the lords, and upon all the people that were therein. So the dead which he slew at his death were more than they which he slew in his life. (Judges 16:30)

Paul (Saul)

Paul was destined to be a preacher unto the Gentiles. He even stated it when he stood before King Agrippa:

15 And I said, Who art thou, Lord? And he said, I am Jesus whom thou persecutest. 16 But rise, and stand upon thy feet: for I have appeared unto thee for this purpose, to make thee a minister and a witness both of these things which thou hast seen, and of those things in the which I will appear unto thee; 17 Delivering thee from the people, and from the Gentiles, unto whom now I send thee, 18 To open their eyes, and to turn them from darkness to light, and from the power of Satan unto God, that they may receive forgiveness of sins, and inheritance among them which are sanctified by faith that is in me. (Acts 26:15-18)

Although Paul slaughtered many men and women of God out of ignorance, he had a heart to do God's service. God knew who Paul was before Paul knew who Paul was. Paul operated under perverted knowledge of Jesus Christ...one that killed the people of God instead of bringing sinners to salvation and deliverance. He was truly converted after his Damascus road experience. When there is true conversion, perversion will certainly be dispelled. Many people became converted under Paul's ministry.

Moses

Moses' divine purpose and destiny began in an ark floating down the Nile River (Exodus 2:1-5). He was born specifically to lead the children of Israel out of the hands of the Egyptians.

10 Come now therefore, and I will send thee unto Pharaoh, that thou mayest bring forth my people the children of Israel out of Egypt. 11 And Moses said unto God, Who am I, that I should go unto Pharaoh, and that I should bring forth the children of Israel out of Egypt? (Exodus 3:10-11).

Moses became angry one day and killed an Egyptian when he saw him abusing a Hebrew. This happened before he discovered that he would be the one to lead his own people out of Egyptian bondage. Weakness in man has never stopped God from using man. Although

Moses murdered a man, Paul went about persecuting the church, and Peter was an attempted murderer, God found no issue with using them to fulfill a purpose that included saving people and nations. Before they were born, God knew that Moses would slay an Egyptian; He knew Paul would be responsible for the murder of God's people; He knew that Samson would love women of the world and would lose his life because of one of them; He knew that Peter would attempt to kill a man for insulting Jesus, yet, they were all used of God to fulfill a purpose in the earth. Jesus chose these men to carry out a mission of which they considered themselves unworthy.

Queen Esther

Esther was chosen by the king to be his queen after Queen Vashti refused to obey an order to come before him. God placed Esther in a position to save the Jews from total annihilation. Things that happen to us are not only about us, but about the will of God for His people.

13 Then Mordecai commanded to answer Esther, Think not with thyself that thou shalt escape in the king's house, more than all the Jews. 14 For if thou altogether holdest thy peace at this time, then shall there enlargement and deliverance arise to the Jews from another place; but thou and thy father's house shall be destroyed: and who knoweth whether thou art come to the kingdom for such a time as this? (Esther 4:13, 14)

Mary (Mother of Jesus)

Mary had a purpose that most women in her day envied, and that the entire Jewish community was awaiting. She was born to carry in her womb and give birth to the Savior of the world, a birth that will forever remain a marvel.

20 But while he thought on these things, behold, the angel of the LORD appeared unto him in a dream, saying, Joseph, thou son of David, fear not to take unto thee Mary thy wife: for that which is conceived in her is of the Holy Ghost. 21 And she shall bring forth a son, and thou shalt call his name JESUS: for he shall save his people from their sins. (Matthew 1:20, 21).

Everyone has a divine purpose for which they were born. Men and women were strategically placed in positions to perform certain tasks and to fulfill certain mandates by God. It is up to us to seek God for His purpose for our lives, and to know what His promises are to us, and then let Him transition us from those promises to fulfillment.

➤ **Power Point!** *Weakness in man has never stopped God from using man.*

Divine Destiny and Purpose

In the past I wondered why I am here-
In this ghastly world of horror and fear-
Never regretting the day I was born,
Cause the reason is thoughtless and so forlorn-

I wanted to know why life exists-
On a planet so filled with a dusty mist;
I related my dreams with a place so divine-
Where people are genuine, honest, and kind;

As I lived throughout each troublesome day-
Worries and wishes led the way;
I tried to find some peace of mind-
I fought vigorously to leave my past behind.

I hoped someday to understand-
Why God created mortal man;
I tried to convey the reason why-
All who sin will surely die.

But now that I know my true destiny-
And since the day Christ set me free-
I no longer wonder why I am here-
Cause my purpose in life God has made very clear.

Queen Kirkwood-Hatchett

12

MAJOR ELEMENTS OF TRANSITION

Transition does not always come easy, and may seem hard and cruel most of the time. Some elements may include:

Pain: Pain is a most precious part of life. One thing that pain will do is cause us to take action, (whether positive or negative) to resolve an issue. Pain is a part of life that will be with us until death do us part, be it physical, emotional, or spiritual. Emotional pain inflicted upon us by someone we trust or love can cause bitterness. It can even cause anger, in which anger can lead to hate, and hate will destroy.

Pain can come from within or without. In Joseph's case, it came from both entities. Imagine being a teenager with very close emotional ties to your father, then, suddenly, you're sold into a strange land by your siblings. Being taken from his homeland must have been a very devastating experience for Joseph. Not only was he taken from his father and his homeland, he was taken from his culture and forced to embrace a new and different one. Strangers and enemies who do not love you and sell you out are one thing, but when your family does it, it adds a new dimension to the pain.

Rejection: Pain from the feeling of rejection can be very excruciating. The impact of rejection depends on the direction from which it comes. To be rejected by co-workers or colleagues is one thing; however, to be rejected by mother, father, siblings, or other people who are dear to our hearts add another element to the pain. The spirit of rejection breeds feelings of isolation; it can create issues of low self-esteem; and if we are not convinced of who we are, it can dominate who God has said we are. Like Jesus, Joseph's own rejected him, but Joseph's father loved and affirmed him before he was sold into slavery, just as God loved and affirmed Jesus before He had his wilderness experience. Joseph and his father shared a very close relationship in which Joseph felt very secure. The relationship that Joseph shared with his father, no doubt, supported and sustained him during his years of crisis in Egypt.

Temptation: Temptation is a part of life that we will constantly face as we live, move, and have our being. Jesus dealt with it when He walked the earth. Joseph's integrity, character, and personality were all on the line when he was tempted by Potiphar's wife. He suffered dearly because he did not give in to temptation but the payoff was great in the end. The three areas in which we are tempted are the lust of the eyes, the lust of the flesh, and the pride of life *(I John 2:16)*. Succumbing to any one of these areas can bring about absolute and total devastation.

Setbacks: Setbacks can be very discouraging during transition. But God has told us that all things work together for our good if we love God and we are called according to His purpose (Romans 8:28). In Joseph's case, his setback was a setup to the palace. Instead of falling into a deep depression or becoming bitter toward Potiphar and his wife when he was put in prison, Joseph exercised his God-given gift. He interpreted the dreams of the butler and the baker. The lesson in this is that when we are at our lowest, God will always come through. Outside of hell and death, Joseph was in the lowest state in which a man can find himself. The worse the condition, the greater the glory! This was proven true with Joseph because it was in prison that God elevated him. It wasn't until he was at the lowest point of his life that he came before the king, and that was when destiny kicked in and took charge.

Ridicule: Joseph was ridiculed, not for dreaming, but for what he dreamed. His brothers mocked him, laughed at him, and ridiculed him at the thought that they would someday bow to him. He was next to the youngest child of the family and they thought that there was no way Joseph could ever become ruler of the clan. The oldest son, Reuben was in line for the chief position. But it is good to know that God chooses whom He will to do His good pleasure, and He chose Joseph before the foundation of the world to rule as governor of Egypt. There was no stopping the plan. Joseph could have had the last laugh, but instead of using the laughing approach, he humbled himself and kept his family alive during the famine. The brothers who sold him were the ones who were mocked in the end.

God has a way of turning the tide, humbling the arrogant, and making others turn their heads and take notice. He has a way of exalting those who others feel are unworthy. He is known to drop the bomb on a situation. Jesus was mocked, "Hail, King of the Jews." (Mark 15:18). Though the Jews meant it sarcastically, Jesus *was*, in fact, King of the Jews. He was not only King of the Jews, but he was **the** King then, now, and forever. Just as Joseph, those who mocked Jesus will surely someday bow to Him.

Disappointment: How disappointed Joseph must have been when his brothers sold him! How disappointed he must have been when he was falsely accused of rape! He had worked around Potiphar's wife for a long time and her husband trusted him. He never misled her in thinking that there was a remote chance they could sleep together. How, then, could this thing happen? In this life, there are appointments and there are disappointments.

Satan is on a mission to take us off course, blur our visions, and assassinate our dreams. He would like to wear out our patience. His desire is to cloud our minds with displaced hope. He wants to cripple our ambitions and cause us to give up on God's promises. He wants us to feel disappointed with God and bring us to total despair. God is ever present to bring back that spark of hope when we feel that we have come to the end of our day. In prison, Joseph's gift came back to life. He had not dreamed since he left Canaan, as far as we know from scripture. When the enemy thinks he has won, God always come through and prove to us who is **really** running the show. When satan thought he had Jesus and the whole world under his power, Jesus rose from the grave and sent satan and his demons running for cover.

When God has appointed us to a certain destiny, the element of disappointment is imminent, but it is merely another element of transition.

A Sentiment of Hope

When it seems there is nothing in life to live for,
And the trials of life you can't take anymore;
When you feel you have failed every time that you tried,
And your passion, hope, and dreams have died;

Take courage, look up, and be of good cheer-
The morning will come and joy will appear;
The sun will shine, and its beautiful beams-
Will restore your passion, hope, and dream.

Queen Kirkwood-Hatchett

➢ **Power Point!** *God is ever present to bring back that spark of hope when we feel that we have come to the end of our day.*

13

ELEMENTS OF A SUCCESSFUL AND TIMELY TRANSITION

We are continuously going through transitions as Christians. We need to know that there are certain requirements to a smooth transition. Transitioning timely does not mean that there won't be some severe tests, and some seemingly unrelenting trials, but it does mean that there are certain actions that can disturb the transition. Transitioning in a timely manner is that on which the children of Israel missed out. They wandered relentlessly for forty years because of their constant and consistent murmuring and complaining.

Listed below are some principles that will help us in making a timely transition from one place or state to another:

1. Always go with the flow of God

God is the pilot and we are not in charge of the flight. God does not demand that we understand what He tells us, but to believe and obey. The landing will be successful as long as God is in the pilot's seat, no matter what happens during the flight.

⁸For my thoughts are not your thoughts, neither are your ways my ways, saith the Lord. ⁹For as the heavens are higher than the earth, so are my ways higher than your ways, and my thoughts than your thoughts. (Isaiah 55:8, 9)

2. Give thanks and praise unto God at all times because it shows unremitting faith in Him; and faith pleases Him.

Murmuring and complaining will only slow the process, displease God, and show signs of unbelief and lack of faith.

³² But as for you, your carcases, they shall fall in this wilderness. ³³ And your children shall wander in the wilderness forty years, and bear your whoredoms, until your carcases be wasted in the wilderness. ³⁴ After the number of the days in which ye searched the land, even forty days, each day for a year, shall ye bear your iniquities, even forty years, and ye shall know my breach of promise. (Numbers 14:32-34)

Not that I speak in respect of want: for I have learned, in whatsoever state I am, therewith to be content. (Philippians 4:11)

But without faith it is impossible to please him: for he that cometh to God must believe that he is, and that he is a rewarder of them that diligently seek him. (Hebrews 11:6)

Let us come before his presence with thanksgiving, and make a joyful noise unto him with psalms. (Psalms 95:2)

3. Forgive those who we feel have harmed us as we are going through.

If we do not forgive others, God will not forgive us. Joseph forgave his brothers as he acknowledged that the enemy meant evil when his brothers sold him; he acknowledged that God wanted to save the ones who meant evil against him.

[14] For if ye forgive men their trespasses, your heavenly Father will also forgive you: [15] But if ye forgive not men their trespasses, neither will your Father forgive your trespasses. (Matthew 6:14, 15)

4. All things are working together.

Sometimes we look into our situations with our analytical and intellectual minds and wonder how the evil, cruel, hurting, or painful things possibly work for our good. Well, that is not our business. That business belongs to God! Our business is to follow God, trust Him, and bless Him at all times.

And we know that all things work together for good to them that love God, to them who are the called according to his purpose. (Romans 8:28)

5. God is forever present.

As we move from transition to transition, there will be times when we may feel that we are alone. Sometimes we may feel that we are cursed and that God has actually turned His back on us. We may even feel that God does not love us. These are all human emotions and have happened with others throughout Bible history. God had to constantly remind His people that He was ever present. God obviously knew that during this journey we would be faced with such thoughts and emotions, so, He went before us and inspired Paul to put pen to paper and encourage us with these words:

Let your conversation be without covetousness; and be content with such things as ye have: for he hath said, I WILL NEVER LEAVE THEE, NOR FORSAKE THEE. (Hebrews 13:5)

Before God inspired the writer to encourage us with Hebrews 13:5, Jesus told us these very words after His resurrection:

...and, lo, I am with you alway, even unto the end of the world. (Matthew 28:20)

6. We must trust God that we are triumphant in Him.

Although we may feel overwhelmed with grief, pain, hurt, sickness, and other challenges, God will never allow a test or trial to overtake us. Victory and success are the only outcomes guaranteed us as children of God...defeat is not in the script.

There hath no temptation taken you but such as is common to man: but God is faithful, who will not suffer you to be tempted above that ye are able; but will with the temptation also make a way to escape, that ye may be able to bear it. (I Corinthians 10:13)

Now thanks be unto God, which always causeth us to triumph in Christ, and maketh manifest the savour of his knowledge by us in every place. (2 Corinthians 2:14)

During Joseph's transition from promise to fulfillment, he did not have the Bible as a blueprint to show him the way. He did not have the Holy Spirit on the inside of Him to lead and guide him into all truth. He did not have the privilege of his father's counseling to instruct him through the tough times in Egypt; yet, he transitioned without blemish. Joseph came out of his final transition smelling like a rose. No debris from his past connected him to his destiny. Only those things that gave glory to God followed Joseph into his final transition.

7. Pray without ceasing.

Prayer is the key to all things. In prayer, God gives instructions, directions, and revelation. Without these elements, we are lost and don't know what to do or where to go. God will always meet his people in prayer. Prayer is our only verbal communication with God. Communication with God is analogous with communication in marriage. Married people will never know what the other is thinking or planning unless they communicate with each other. Intimacy involves talking and not just sexing. If we are intimate with God, we will tell Him exactly what we feel, how we feel, our desires, and we will hold nothing back from Him. We will come before Him naked, exposed, and hiding nothing. On the other hand, God will share His heart with us and tell us all that we need to know and do in order to please Him and to be successful in our walk with Him. He will hold nothing back from us. No marriage has ever been successful without total communication. Communication is a must in any union between two people. A relationship with any substance depends on total communication. The Bible tells us to pray...and not just occasionally:

And he spake a parable unto them to this end, that men ought always to pray, and not to faint; (Luke 18:1)

Pray without ceasing. (I Thessalonians 5:17)

Watch and pray, that ye enter not into temptation: the spirit indeed is willing, but the flesh is weak. (Matthew 26:41)

> ➤ **Power Point!** *God does not command that we understand what He tells us, but to believe and obey.*

14

THE CUCUMBERS, MELONS, LEEKS, ONIONS AND GARLICK SYNDROME

W hile reading and studying the children of Israel's journey through the wilderness, it was quite interesting to note that they only murmured and complained at certain times. It was noticeable that they murmured and complained when things didn't go their way and when they came to a point in the wilderness where it seemed as though they were trapped. These were also the times they spoke about going back to Egypt. In the following passages, they spoke about their "soul" being dried.

⁵ We remember the fish, which we did eat in Egypt freely; the cucumbers, and the melons, and the leeks, and the onions, and the garlick: ⁶ But now our soul is dried away: there is nothing at all, beside this manna, before our eyes. (Numbers 11:5, 6)

And the children of Israel said unto them, Would to God we had died by the hand of the LORD in the land of Egypt, when we sat by the flesh pots, and when we did eat bread to the full; for ye have brought us forth into this wilderness, to kill this whole assembly with hunger. (Exodus 16:3)

The children of Israel were feeling unfulfilled because their appetite was driven by things of the world. Their flesh was calling for things of the past. They had left their comfort zone in Egypt.

Although they were living the best life ever, as we can see from reading the scriptures, they were not accustomed to being free. Bondage was their comfort zone and anything outside of that was "the unknown" to them. They were only familiar with the leeks, onions, garlick, melons, and of course, bondage. They even complained about the bread that the Almighty God rained down from heaven for them. As we read these scriptures, we can see how the enemy had the children of Israel blinded about their new life.

If things were so good for them while they were in Egypt, why had they prayed for over 400 years for God to deliver them out of the hands of Pharaoh? Also, if things were all that wonderful for them while they were in Egypt, why didn't they stay in Egypt instead of following Moses across the Red Sea? There is more going on here than meets the eye! The enemy wanted to keep their mind in Egypt in hope that their bodies would follow.

When things seemed hard for them, the enemy brought the smell of onions, leeks, melons, and garlick to their noses to remind them from whence they came. Notice the things that the enemy brought to their minds about Egypt. They said that food was there – something that would only feed the flesh and would make their bellies full. The enemy never reminded them of how they suffered under the hands of Pharaoh or how Pharaoh had killed thousands of their ancestors and had them held captive and in bondage for hundreds of years. The enemy would not allow them to feel the pain of the whips on their backs. He did not let them see or think about the many days and nights they could not spend with their loved ones or enjoy their children and grandchildren because of the hard labor. Neither did the enemy allow them to see that no one had ever been as good to them as God.

21 And the LORD went before them by day in a pillar of a cloud, to lead them the way; and by night in a pillar of fire, to give them light; to go by day and night: 22 He took not away the pillar of the cloud by day, nor the pillar of fire by night, from before the people. (Exodus 13:21-22).

And the children of Israel did eat manna forty years, until they came to a land inhabited; they did eat manna, until they came unto the borders of the land of Canaan. (Exodus 16:35)

⁵And I have led you forty years in the wilderness: your clothes are not waxen old upon you, and thy shoe is not waxen old upon thy foot. ⁶ Ye have not eaten bread, neither have ye drunk wine or strong drink: that ye might know that I am the LORD your God. (Deuteronomy 29:5-6)

Fear of the unknown gripped their hearts when they came to a point where they needed food or water. They also complained when they had been given a word that God was going to deliver them from Egypt. Pharaoh put pressure on them after Moses told him what God said about releasing them. Sometimes the enemy challenges the word that we get from God, and the purpose is to instill fear in our hearts. Pharaoh punished them because of what Moses said to him. That is the way the enemy works! He gets highly upset when the Lord has declared our victory.

Things about which the children of Israel murmured and complained were things that the flesh required. We must be very careful and alert during transition that we do not let the cucumbers, melons, leeks, and onions pull our minds back into the world while we are going through hard trials and tests. There is nothing attractive about the world that should cause us to want to go back.

Murmuring and complaining about what is happening in our lives can cause us to wander aimlessly in transition and prolong our destiny in God; not only that, but it displeases God and shows no appreciation for what He has already done in our lives. Furthermore, it demonstrates that we are discrediting God's ability to perform in our lives and bring to pass His promises.

➢ **Power Point!** *We must be aware and beware during transition that we do not allow the cucumbers, melons, leeks, and onions to pull our minds back into the world while we are going through hard trials and tests.*

15

THE GREATEST TRANSITION OF ALL

N o one can debate the fact that Jesus' transitions were the greatest and most powerful ever. The first transition phase, conception to birth, was the most phenomenal that man has ever known and will ever know.

But while he thought on these things, behold, the angel of the Lord appeared unto him in a dream, saying, Joseph, thou son of David, fear not to take unto thee Mary thy wife: for that which is conceived in her is of the Holy Ghost. (Matthew 1:20).

And he knew her not til she had brought forth her firstborn son: and he called his name JESUS. (Matthew 1:25)

[12] But as many as received him, to them gave he power to become the sons of God, even to them that believe on his name: [13] Which were born, not of blood, nor of the will of the flesh, nor of the will of man, but of God. [14] And the Word was made flesh, and dwelt among us, (and we beheld his glory, the glory as of the only begotten of the Father,) full of grace and truth. (John 1:12-14)

Jesus' blood was not contaminated, but was pure and unblemished. If he had been born from the seed of man, His blood would have been polluted. Man's blood is contaminated because it carries in it the element or DNA of Adam's sin. For this reason, God wrapped Himself in flesh, entered Mary's womb, and at the proper time she gave birth to Jesus, the Son of God, our Redeemer and our Salvation.

In the second transitional phase of Jesus' life on earth, He began his ministry. He was baptized and began His ministry at the age of thirty.

[21] Now when all the people were baptized, it came to pass, that Jesus also being baptized, and praying, the heaven was opened, [22] And the Holy Ghost descended in a bodily shape like a dove upon him, and a voice came from heaven, which said, Thou art my beloved Son; in thee I am well pleased. [23] And Jesus himself began to be about thirty years of age, being (as was supposed) the son of Joseph, which was the son of Heli, (Luke 3:21-23)

It was during this second phase that Jesus experienced much agonizing pain and suffering; the most horrible ever experienced and endured by man. During this second transitional phase of human life, he was:

Despised
He is despised and rejected of men...; (Isaiah 53:3)

Denied

(Matthew 26:69-75)
[69] Now Peter sat without in the palace: and a damsel came unto him, saying, Thou also wast with Jesus of Galilee. [70] But he denied before them all, saying, I know not what thou sayest. [71] And when he was gone out into the porch, another maid saw him, and said unto them that were there, This fellow was also with Jesus of Nazareth. [72] And again he denied with an oath, I do not know the man. [73] And after a while came unto him they that stood by, and said to Peter, Surely

thou also art one of them; for thy speech betrayeth thee. [74] *Then began he to curse and to swear, saying, I know not the man. And immediately the cock crew.* [75] *And Peter remembered the word of Jesus, which said unto him, Before the cock crow, thou shalt deny me thrice. And he went out, and wept bitterly.*

Betrayed

[41] *And he cometh the third time, and saith unto them, Sleep on now, and take your rest: it is enough, the hour is come; behold, the Son of man is betrayed into the hands of sinners.* [42] *Rise up, let us go; lo, he that betrayeth me is at hand. (Mark 14:41, 42)*

Rejected

He is despised and rejected of men; a man of sorrows, and acquainted with grief: and we hid as it were our faces from him; he was despised, and we esteemed him not. (Isaiah 53:3)

Wounded and bruised

But he was wounded for our transgressions, he was bruised for our iniquities: the chastisement of our peace was upon him; and with his stripes we are healed. (Isaiah 53:5)

Scourged

Then released he Barabbas unto them: and when he had scourged Jesus, he delivered him to be crucified. (Matthew 27:26)

Spat Upon

And they spit upon him, and took the reed, and smote him on the head. (Matthew 27:30)

Pierced

And I will pour upon the house of David, and upon the inhabitants of Jerusalem, the spirit of grace and of supplications: and they shall look upon me whom they have pierced, and they shall mourn for him, as one mourneth for his only son, and shall be in bitterness for him, as one that is in bitterness for his firstborn. (Zechariah 12:10)

But one of the soldiers with a spear pierced his side, and forthwith came there out blood and water. (John 19:34)

Mocked
For he shall be delivered unto the Gentiles, and shall be mocked, and spitefully entreated, and spitted on: (Luke 18:32)

And the men that held Jesus mocked him, and smote him. (Luke 22:63)

And Herod with his men of war set him at nought, and mocked him, and arrayed him in a gorgeous robe, and sent him again to Pilate. (Luke 23:11)

Smitten
[67] Then did they spit in his face, and buffeted him; and others smote him with the palms of their hands, [68] Saying, Prophesy unto us, thou Christ, Who is he that smote thee: (Matthew 26:67, 68).

And they smote him on the head with a reed, and did spit upon him, and bowing their knees worshipped him. (Mark 15:19)

Accused of Blasphemy
Then the high priest rent his clothes, saying, He hath spoken blasphemy; what further need have we of witnesses? Behold, now ye have heard his blasphemy. (Matthew 26:65)

The Jews answered him, saying, For a good work we stone thee not; but for blasphemy; and because that thou, being a man, makest thyself God. (John 10:33)

Accused of being a devil
Then answered the Jews, and said unto him, Say we not well that thou art a Samaritan, and hast a devil? (John 8:48)

And many of them said, He hath a devil, and is mad; why hear ye him? (John 10:20)

Crucified
[17] And he bearing his cross went forth into a place called the place of a skull, which is called in the Hebrew Golgotha: [18] Where they crucified him, and two other with him, on either side one, and Jesus in the midst. (John 19:17, 18)

Jesus, when he had cried with a loud voice, yielded up the ghost. (Matthew 27:50)

Therefore doth my Father love me, because I lay down my life, that I might take it again. No man taketh it from me, but I lay it down of myself. I have power to lay it down, and I have power to take it again. This commandment have I received of my Father. (John 10:17, 18)

After giving up the ghost, Jesus entered into the third and final transitional phase of life; physical death. We know, however, that Jesus existed even in the beginning. He went into the grave only for a season.

Jesus said unto them, Verily, verily, I say unto you, Before Abraham was, I am. (John 8:58)

However, the manifestation of his physical being suffered much pain during his short time on earth and he endured an agonizing death on the cross. After appearing to his disciples and giving some final commands, He ascended up into heaven.

⁹ And when he had spoken these things, while they beheld, he was taken up; and a cloud received him out of their sight. ¹⁰ And while they looked stedfastly toward heaven as he went up, behold, two men stood by them in white apparel; ¹¹ Which also said, Ye men of Galilee, why stand ye gazing up into heaven? this same Jesus, which is taken up from you into heaven, shall so come in like manner as ye have seen him go into heaven. (Acts 1:9-11)

What a glorious day it will be when Jesus descends from heaven! Just as He rose from the grave, we will rise, just as he ascended, we will ascend; just as he lives, we will live forever. What a wonderful hope we have in Christ!

The second phase of Jesus' transition is the phase that we, who are alive, are experiencing. During this transition, we have been encouraged to "endure hardness as a good soldier of Jesus Christ" (2 Timothy 2:3). We have been promised that if we suffer, we shall also reign with Him (2 Timothy 2:12).

Some of us will not see death at the final transition, but there will surely be a third transition. Whether we experience transition in the rapture or through physical death, we **will** experience a third transition.

⁵¹ Behold, I shew you a mystery; We shall not all sleep, but we shall all be changed, ⁵² In a moment, in the twinkling of an eye, at the last trump: for the trumpet shall sound, and the dead shall be raised incorruptible, and we shall be changed.⁵³ For this corruptible must put on incorruption, and this mortal must put on immortality. (I Corinthians 15:51-53)

The question concerning the third transition is whether we reign with Jesus or transition to a place of torment. My friends, I don't know about you, but knowing that there will surely be a final transition, I am preparing to reign with Jesus.

> ➢ **Power Point!** *No one can debate that Jesus' transitions were the greatest and most powerful ever known to man.*

HE LIVES

No man could have suffered the agony-
No man could have withstood the misery-
Or the pain and affliction on Calvary-
That Jesus endured to set men free.

He was stricken, betrayed, afflicted and denied,
Rejected, smitten, bruised, and despised;
He was tried, convicted, and whipped all night long;
But Jesus, the Savior, had done no wrong.

They platted a crown of thorns on his head-
"Hail, King of the Jews," they sarcastically said;
They scourged the Savior and spat in his face-
Then they led Him up that ghastly place.

He was nailed to the cross and pierced in the side-
Our Lord and Savior was crucified;
They buried His body but He rose again-
Declaring all power in heaven and earth in His hands.

His blood was shed for all mankind-
For the healing of the spirit, soul, body, and mind;
He's the way, the truth, the life, and the door;
He is alive now, and forevermore!

Queen Kirkwood-Hatchett

16

THE FINAL TRANSITION

I was privileged to witness the birth of my third grandson, Josiah. Many thoughts entered my mind in anticipation of his long awaited birth.

Josiah was travelling to the outside world while my daughter was pushing in agonizing pain and travail. The doctor, at this point, was in the chief position. He sat directly in front of her as she lay in the undeviating positon to give birth. The nurses were in position and waiting for commands from the doctor. Friends and loved ones were all awaiting the news of Josiah's birth.

Those who were in the delivery room knew that the baby was near home when the top of his head became visible. The last resilient push by his mother landed the baby in the hands of the doctor. The doctor gave him a full examination and passed him on to the nurses so they could perform their duties. My grandson had finally transitioned from the womb to the other side; to the place where many people were awaiting his arrival, and the place that he would spend his second transition.

Transitioning from this life to the next is inevitable. It will happen whether we are ready or not. It is not up to us to remain in this life forever. It is not a matter of whether it will happen, but when it will happen.

As I witnessed Josiah's transition and arrival, I was reminded of what is going to happen when Jesus returns. Josiah, my grandson, slept and breathed one last night in his mother's womb, then, all of a sudden he was in the hands of the doctor. One day, we will say our last word, breathe our last breath, sleep our last night, eat our last meal, and close our eyes one last time on this earth. Then, all of a sudden, we will be in the place that we have been anticipating for so long. We will be with our Lord and Savior, Jesus Christ.

The body will go back to the dust, the spirit will go back to God, and the soul will go to a place of torment, or, it will go to be with Jesus. At the final resurrection, and just as the doctor was there to catch my grandson and make sure that he transitioned with no outside forces to interrupt, Jesus will be there to welcome those who have accepted Him as their Lord and Savior, who have walked upright before Him and obeyed His Word. Those who have not given their lives to Christ will be welcomed by satan and his hordes. A final judgment will be made on both ends and everyone will embrace their final transition, which will be everlasting life.

When most people think of everlasting life, they only think of everlasting life with Jesus Christ. Everyone will experience everlasting life, but unfortunately, everyone will not spend it with Jesus Christ. Those who accept Jesus Christ as their personal Savior will spend everlasting life with Him. In great opposition to that, those who choose to live an ungodly life will also experience everlasting life, but it will be spent in everlasting damnation.

For those who have not given their lives to Jesus Christ, I strongly recommend that you do so today; and do it with the quickness. Time is of the essence! We do not know the exact day or hour that Jesus will return for His people, but we do know that it is vastly approaching. My plea is that you accept Jesus Christ as your Lord and Savior, ask Him to forgive your sins and come into your life, sit on the throne of your heart, and guide your life from this point on. He will forgive your sins, wash you clean, fill you with His Spirit, and make you whole again-He is waiting for us to call on His name.

That if thou shalt confess with thy mouth the Lord Jesus, and shalt believe in thine heart that God hath raised him from the dead, thou shalt be saved. (Romans 10:9)

37 Now when they heard this, they were pricked in their heart, and said unto Peter and to the rest of the apostles, Men and brethren, what shall we do? 38 Then Peter said unto them, Repent, and be baptized every one of you in the name of Jesus Christ for the remission of sins, and ye shall receive the gift of the Holy Ghost. (Acts 2:37, 38)

Once you have received Jesus Christ as your Lord and Savior, you become a new creature.

Therefore, if any man be in Christ, he is a new creature: old things are passed away; behold, all things are become new. (2 Corinthians 5:17)

It does not take God hours, weeks, months or years to forgive sins. Once you ask him from a sincere heart, it is done.

➢ **Power Point!** *Transitioning from this life to the next is inevitable.*

CONCLUSION

Transition is as sure as death and taxes and we will experience both in this life. Every transition is specifically designed with distinct trials and tests that are highly essential to destiny. Joseph had his share of experiences in transition. After God showed Joseph his destiny, he experienced three levels of transition. His first transition was from his homeland to a foreign land. The second transition was from Potiphar's house to prison. His third and final transition was from the prison to the palace; there he ruled as governor.

The first and second transitions positioned him for his destiny. As we can see, his destiny was to deliver his family and Egypt from perishing in the famine. I am quite sure that at the time of his transitions, Joseph did not foresee the outcome; however, God had already determined his end from his beginning. When he transitioned to Potiphar's house, he experienced his one major test when Potiphar's wife tried to seduce him into having sex with her.

Everything from his living arrangement to his diet changed when he entered Egypt. Each of his transitions resulted in a different circle of associates and different trials and tests. His circle of associates was other slaves when he first landed in Egypt. His circle of associates became other prisoners when he was imprisoned. His circle of associates shifted from a circle of slaves and prisoners to a circle of people of royalty, honor, and prestige when he transitioned from prisoner to governor.

God truly got the glory out of Joseph's life from his entry into Egypt to his position of governor. Every level of transition that he experienced caused the name of God to be exalted. He did nothing to bring shame or embarrassment to the name of his heavenly Master or his earthly master.

Many people saw Joseph when he first arrived in Egypt. They came to know him when he was just a teenager. They saw him as he transitioned from a teenager to a full-grown man. They witnessed his transition from prisoner to governor. His name was never tarnished, his reputation remained unpolluted, and he consistently demonstrated humility during his transitions. Many, no doubt, heard of the accusations made against Joseph by Potiphar's wife and they knew of his imprisonment. Knowing his character as they did, my assessment is that some doubted that the accusation was true.

When Joseph reached his high ground, he brought glory to his God. His success in Egypt came not by pulling strings, brown-nosing, lying, cheating, manipulating, playing games, or fighting against his master, but his success came by:

- ✓ Holding his peace when he could have spoken out
- ✓ Standing tall when all of the odds seemed as if they were stacked against him
- ✓ Knowing who he was although he was enslaved and in a strange land
- ✓ Forgiving his enemies
- ✓ Having the divine favor of God upon his life
- ✓ Giving glory to God
- ✓ Honoring Potiphar and Pharaoh

Joseph withstood the test of time as he endured captivity in Egypt and he was greatly rewarded in the end. He was given double for his trouble. When God finally brought him face to face with destiny, He did it "suddenly."

We experience many elements of life as we go through transitions. Some experiences are positive and make us very happy, and some are not so pleasant or smooth and they make us very sad; however, they are all strategically designed to work for our spiritual growth and development. The ultimate conclusion is that God will be glorified. Every level of transition that we go through is intended to bring glory to God in the end.

> ➢ **Power Point!** Every transition is specifically designed with distinct trials and tests that are highly essential to our destinies.

The Confession of a King (A Lesson of Humility)
(Daniel 4)

This poem is a reminder of what can happen when we refuse to submit and be humble under God's mighty hand in any circumstance. Humility is the way to go!

Nebuchadnezzar's my name and when I was king-
I did not honor God; I did my own thing.
My kingdom was awesome; it was second to none,
My army was great; many battles I won.

But one night while asleep on my palace bed-
A most terrible dream came to by head;
So to the wise men of Babylon I made a decree-
To make known the interpretation of the dream to me.

They could not interpret just what the dream meant-
So, for the magicians, enchanters and astrologers I sent;
They, too, failed to make known to me what it meant,
So, for Daniel, the prophet of God I sent.

My dream was this, O Daniel, I said-
As I slept that night on my palace bed:
In the midst of the earth I saw a tall, strong tree-
Its heights reached the heavens and all could see.

It yielded much fruit, and the leaves were so fair!
In the boughs of the tree dwelt the fowls of the air;
In the shade of the tree rested all the wild beasts-
There was truly meat for all flesh to feast.

I continued to dream as I lay on my bed-
A Watcher and Holy One came from heaven and said;
"Cut down the tree; cut the branches off, too-
Shake the leaves off the tree and scatter the fruit;

Let the beasts get from under the shade of the tree-
And he said for the fowls in the branches to flee;
Leave the stump of his roots with a band of iron and brass-
And let it be surrounded by the tender grass.

Let him have his portion with the beasts of the grass-
And have the mind of an animal 'til seven years pass.
This is a matter of the watcher's decree-
The Holy One has demanded this thing to be."

Daniel was astonished for one hour, then said-
"'Tis the meaning of the dream you saw in your head:
The tree which was strong that grew and grew-
'Til its heights reached the heaven, O King, was you.

Thy kingdom, O King, is very well known,
To the ends of the earth thy greatness has grown;
But now the Most High has made a decree-
That all of these things shall come upon thee.

They shall drive you from men, and your dwelling shall be-
With the beasts of the field-and they shall make thee-
To eat grass like an oxen, and wet shall thou be-
With the dew from heaven-'Tis the decree.

Seven years will pass and you will know then-
That the Most High ruleth in the kingdom of men-
And He giveth it to whomsoever He will.
You will return to your kingdom when this is fulfilled.

Let my counsel, O King, be acceptable to thee,
And break off thy sins and iniquities;
Show righteousness, and to the poor, mercy,
And there may be a lengthening of your prosperity."

Exactly one year passed after Daniel's prophecy,
Then all of these things did come upon me:
I was walking on the roof of my palace in Babylon-
Giving glory to myself for work I had done.

I was lauding myself and speaking boastful words-
When a voice from heaven I immediately heard;
These are the words that it said to me:
"Your kingdom, O King is departed from thee.

They shall drive you from men and your dwelling shall be-
With the beasts of the field, and they shall make thee-
To eat grass like an oxen and wet shall thou be-
With the dew from heaven – 'Tis the decree.

Seven years will pass and you will know then-
That the Most High ruleth in the kingdom of men;
And He giveth it to whomsoever He will.
You will return to your kingdom when this is fulfilled."

So, like the claws on a bird, my nails they grew-
My body was drenched with heaven's dew;
I ate my portion with the beasts in the grass-
This was my estate 'til seven years passed.

Then, I looked up to heaven and my sanity returned,
I blessed the Most High and to reverence Him, I learned.
He does as He will at His own command-

And no one can question the works of His hand.
When my sanity returned, my kingdom did, too.
My honor and power were made anew;
My counselors and lords, they sought after me-
I was reestablished in my kingdom with excellent majesty.

I, King Nebuchadnezzar praised and extolled the Most High,
The King of heaven, I did glorify;
His words are truth, and just are His ways-
And those who walk in pride, He is able to abase.

Queen Kirkwood-Hatchett

QUICK STUDY GUIDE

1. **Part 1 – Questions and Answers/Recall**

2. **Part 2 – Questions and Answers/Recall**

3. **Sentence Completion**

Part 1
Questions and Answers

1. Name at least eight examples of how Jesus and Joseph's lives parallel.

A

_____

_____

_____

B

_____

_____

_____

C

_____

_____

_____

D

_____

_____

_____

E

_____

_____

_____

F

_____

_____

_____

G

_____

_____

_____

H

_____

_____

_____

2. What name did Pharaoh give Joseph?

_____

3. List three items that Pharaoh gave Joseph the day he became governor of Egypt.

    Λ _____

    B _____

    C _____

4. What was Potiphar's position in Egypt?

_____

5. Of what crime was Joseph accused?

_____

6. Give the title of the two men who had dreams, the dreams they dreamed, and Joseph's interpretation.

Title _____

Dream

_____
_____
_____
_____
_____
_____

Interpretation

_____
_____
_____
_____
_____
_____

Title _____

Dream

_____
_____
_____
_____
_____
_____

Interpretation

_____

_____

_____

_____

_____

_____

7. List eight main characters in Joseph's life and the roles they played.

Name _____

Role _____

Name _____

Role _____

Name _____

Role _____

Name _____

Role _____

Name _____

Role _____

Name _____

Role _____

Name _____

Role _____

Name _____

Role _____

Part 2
Questions and Answers

1. What is the definition of "transition?"

_____

_____

_____

_____

_____

2. What is the definition of "attitude?"

_____

_____

_____

3. List five dreamers or visionaries of the Old or New Testament.

    A _____

    B _____

    C _____

    D _____

    E _____

4. List five of Joseph's positive characteristics and describe how he portrayed them.

A

_____

_____

_____

_____

_____

B

_____

_____

_____

_____

C

_____

_____

_____

_____

_____

D

_____

_____

_____

_____

_____

E

_____

_____

_____

_____

_____

5. Name three reasons that God uses dreams and visions in the lives of His people.

A _____

B _____

C _____

6. What number was significant in Joseph's life? _____

7. Name five examples of the significant number in Joseph's life.

A _____

B _____

C _____

D _____

E _____

8. Why do you suggest Jacob did not investigate Joseph's disappearance?

_____

_____

_____

_____

_____

9. Out of his twelve sons, it is apparent that Jacob loved Joseph more. How do you describe his respected love?

_____

_____

_____

_____

_____

_____

_____

_____

10. Describe the character of Potiphar's wife.

_____

_____

_____

_____

11. Why do you suppose Joseph chose Simeon to stay in prison in Egypt while the others were released?

_____

_____

_____

_____

_____

_____

12. Name some main events of Joseph's life?

_____

_____

_____

_____

_____

_____

_____

13. Name six major elements of transition as described in chapter twelve.

_____

_____

_____

_____

_____

_____

14. What obstacle/s did Joseph face in Egypt?

_____

_____

_____

_____

_____

_____

15. How did he overcome it/them?

_____

_____

_____

_____

_____

_____

_____

16. Which part of the story of Joseph's life appeals to you the most? Why?

_____

_____

_____

_____

Part 3
Sentence Completion (Found only in Genesis)

Complete the following quotes or fill in the missing word(s) from the story of the life of Joseph in Egypt. Quotes are from the Kings James Version of the Bible.

1. "And when his brethren saw that their father loved him more than all his brethren, they hated him, _____ _____

_____ _____ _____ _____

_____."

2. "And she caught him by his garment, saying _____

_____; and he left his garment in her hand, and

_____, and got him out."

3. "And Pharaoh called Joseph's name _____ ; and he gave him to wife _____ the daughter of Potipherah."

4. "And when all the land of Egypt was famished, the people cried to Pharaoh for bread: and Pharaoh said unto all the Egyptians, _____, _____ _____."

5. "Now therefore _____ _____ _____: I will nourish you, and your little ones."

6. "And he made him to ride in the second chariot which he had; and they cried before him, _____ _____ _____:"

7. "And his brothers envied him; _____ _____
_____ _____ _____ _____."

8. "And for that the dream was doubled unto Pharaoh _____;
it is because the thing is _____ by God, and God will
shortly bring it to pass."

9. "And when they saw him afar off, even before he came unto them,
they _____ against him to slay him."

10. "And he restored the chief butler unto his butlership again;
and he gave the cup into Pharaoh's hand: But _____
_____ _____ _____
_____: as Joseph had interpreted to them."

ANSWER KEY

Part 1
Questions and Answers

1. Answers found in FYI
2. Zaphnathpaaneah
3. a ring, vestures of fine linen, golden chain
4. captain of the guard
5. rape
6. **Butler** – Dreamed of a vine with three branches that budded and blossomed; clusters that brought forth ripe grapes; he pressed wine into the cup and gave it to Pharaoh; the interpretation was that in three days he would be restored to his position with Pharaoh

Baker – Dreamed of three white baskets on his head; the birds ate out of the baskets; the interpretation was that in three days Pharaoh would have him hung on a tree and the birds of the air would eat his flesh.
7. Characters are found throughout the chapters

Part 2
Questions and Answers

1. "transition" is "passage from one state, stage, subject, or place to another; movement, development, or evolution from one form, stage, or style to another".
2. According to the author, "attitude" is "a characterized behavior, whether positive or negative, that responds to an action, a person, an event, a circumstance or a set of circumstances".
3. Joseph (Mary's husband)/Jacob/Gideon/King Solomon/ King Abimelech/Pharaoh/the Wise men/Joseph (of the Old Testament)/Ananias/Paul/Peter/butler/baker/ and others
4. Joseph was honest, loving, forgiving, giving, humble, compassionate
5. Comfort and confirmation/warning/directions and instructions/ prophecy
6. The number 2
7. He had two dreams/interpreted two dreams/he had two sons/in prison two years after interpreting the two dreams/he had two pit experiences
8. Use your own comprehension
9. Use your own comprehension
10. Use your own comprehension
11. Use your own comprehension
12. The answers are in chapters three through eleven
13. Pain/rejection/temptation/setbacks/ridicule/disappointment
14. The answers can be found in the chapters three through eleven
15. Answer according to the answers you found in chapters three through twelve
16. Use your own comprehension

Part 3
Sentence Completion

1. and could not speak peaceably with him
2. lie with me/fled
3. Zaphnathpaaneah/Asenath
4. go unto Joseph
5. fear ye not
6. bow the knee
7. but his father observed the saying
8. twice/established
9. conspired
10. he hanged the chief baker

FYI

Joseph's life is more typical and characteristic of Jesus' than any other Bible character.

- Moses miraculously led the children of Israel out of Egypt and across the Red Sea
- Elijah caused fire to come down from heaven and was taken to heaven in a chariot of fire
- Samson was the strongest man who ever lived
- King David was a man after God's own heart
- Joshua spoke and the sun stood still for one whole day
- Peter defied the laws of nature and walked on water
- Enoch never saw death because he pleased God
- King Solomon was the wisest man who ever lived

No one can dispute the fact that these were great men of God; however, none of their lives are more symbolic of the life of Jesus than that of Joseph. Besides the life of Jesus, the narrative of the life of Joseph is one of the most interesting and extraordinary in the Bible. Let us examine the life of Joseph and observe the parallel.

- **Joseph was despised by his brothers**

And when his brethren saw that their father loved him more than all his brethren, they hated him, and could not speak peaceably unto him. (Genesis 37:4)

Joseph was hated by his brothers because their father loved him more than he loved his other sons, except Benjamin. Jacob loved Joseph more because he was born to him in his old age. Rachel, Joseph's mother was also Jacob's favorite wife. Jacob affirmed Joseph and gave him a coat of many colors to seal his identity and his place of authority in the clan. (Genesis 37:3)

- **Jesus was despised by his own (the Jews)**

He is despised and rejected of men; a man of sorrows, and acquainted with grief: and we hid as it were our faces from him; he was despised, and we esteemed him not. (Isaiah 53:3)

Jesus' own despised him because He claimed to be the Son of God. They also despised Him because of the miracles he performed. The scribes and Pharisees hated Him. Jesus walked and talked in authority because He knew who He was and He knew His purpose. When people walk, talk, speak, act, or work in authority, those who are ignorant and insecure about who they are may become intimidated. Jesus knew who He was because His Father affirmed Him.

And lo a voice from heaven, saying, This is my beloved Son, in whom I am well pleased. (Matthew 3:17)

- **Joseph's brothers conspired to kill him**

And when they saw him afar off, even before he came near unto them, they conspired against him to slay him. (Genesis 37:18)

After Joseph's brothers saw an opportunity to get rid of him, they began their scheme. When they saw him coming, they commented about his dreams and his interpretation that they would bow before him. It is amazing how all hell breaks loose after a prophetic word is spoken over our lives! Joseph had received a prophetic dream from God, and was even mildly rebuked by his father. His future included his family, but to them, it was in a humiliating manner. Reuben was the oldest of the brothers and should have shown a bit more leadership competence in the matter, instead, to a degree, he went along with the plot to a degree. He didn't really want Joseph to die, so he insisted they put him in the pit, hoping he could deliver him later, only to return and discover that Joseph was not there.

- **Jesus' own conspired to kill him**

Then from that day forth they took counsel together for to put him to death. (John 11:53)

Several attempts were made on Jesus' life; however, it was not his time to die *(John 8:58; 10:31; 10:39)*. God instructed Joseph to take Jesus down to Egypt and hide him when he was a child because Herod put a hit out on His life. Joseph had to run just as Jesus did. Running is sometimes the right thing to do and it doesn't mean that there is fear or weakness, but a willingness to do God's will and not to allow people or things to interrupt or cause the mission, plan, and purpose to be aborted or miscarried.

- **Joseph was sold for twenty pieces of silver**

26 And Judah said unto his brethren, What profit is it if we slay our brother, and conceal his blood? 27 Come, and let us sell him to the Ishmeelites, and let not our hand be upon him; for he is our brother and our flesh. And his brethren were content. 28 Then there passed by Midianites merchantmen; and they drew and lifted up Joseph out of the pit, and sold Joseph to the Ishmeelites for twenty pieces of silver: and they brought Joseph into Egypt. (Genesis 37:26-28)

Besides Reuben, Judah was the only brother who came to Joseph's defense. It seems that Judah felt a certain responsibility to try and save Joseph.

- **Jesus was sold for 30 pieces of silver**

[14] Then one of the twelve, called Judas Iscariot, went unto the chief priests, [15] And said unto them, What will ye give me, and I will deliver him unto you? And they covenanted with him for thirty pieces of silver. (Matthew 26:14-15)

Judas discovered in the end that mammon does not satisfy the human soul.

- **Joseph was delivered over to Gentile rulers**

And Joseph was brought down to Egypt; and Potiphar, an officer of Pharaoh, captain of the guard, an Egyptian, bought him of the hands of the Ishmeelites, which had brought him down thither. (Genesis 39:1)

Joseph was sold to Ishmeelite traders who sold him to Potiphar, a Gentile. Joseph's brothers thought they had destroyed him by selling him. Joseph, however, was sent by God to save not only his people from famine, but the Gentiles also. No matter what happened in Joseph's life, even while he was in Egypt, victory and triumph were eminent.

- **Jesus was delivered over to Gentiles rulers**

For he shall be delivered unto the Gentiles, and shall be mocked, and spitefully entreated, and spitted on: (Luke 18:32)

And straightway in the morning the chief priests held a consultation with the elders and scribes and the whole council, and bound Jesus, and carried him away, and delivered him to Pilate. (Mark 15:1)

The Jewish leaders turned Jesus over to the Romans after they paid Judas off. They thought that they were bringing Jesus to his end when they turned him over to the Romans. Nothing takes God by surprise because He is omniscient. Jesus died for the sins of man. He did not come to the earth to live forever. Once He fulfilled His purpose, and His mission was accomplished, He went back to the Father.

- **Joseph was placed under the authority of the strongest army in the world when he was sold**

And the Midianites sold him into Egypt unto Potiphar, an officer of Pharaoh's, and captain of the guard. (Genesis 37:36)

Potiphar was a blessed man because Joseph was in his house (Genesis 39:5). Joseph's destiny was to save the nation of Israel. He not only saved his nation, but he also saved Egypt. The things that we suffer in this life are not always *just* for us. Joseph suffered after his brothers sold him, but at the same time, they needed him to deliver them from famine. It behooves us to be very careful about the way we treat people. The very people we put in a pit may be the very ones to have to pull us out of one.

Jesus was placed under the authority of the Romans, the strongest army at the time he was crucified

And straightway in the morning the chief priests held a consultation with the elders and scribes and the whole council, and bound Jesus, and carried him away, and delivered him to Pilate. (Mark 15:1)

The chief priests had no authority of their own, so they hid behind the Romans.

- **Joseph was sentenced to the king's prison (a type of hell) for a crime he did not commit**

And Joseph's master took him, and put him into the prison, a place where the king's prisoners were bound: and he was there in the prison. (Genesis 39:20)

Joseph was thrown into what we call "federal prison." No matter what position in which we find ourselves, it does not change who we are. Situations do not change who we are, they do not dictate our final destination, and they do not change our position with God, our calling, anointing, or our destiny. All things worked for Joseph while he was in Egypt because he was destined to rule.

- **Jesus went to hell, a type of prison for a crime he did not commit**

He seeing this before spake of the resurrection of Christ, that his soul was not left in hell, neither his flesh did see corruption. (Acts 2:31)

Joseph and Jesus were innocent of all charges brought against them. And when they came out, they came out with great power and authority. Jesus was sentenced to death and He went to hell. He rose with the keys to death and hell, and with all power in his hand. He now sits on the right hand of the Father *(I Peter 3:22)*. Joseph was sentenced to prison but came out with authority over all of Egypt and ruled next to the most powerful man in the world at that time.

- **The jailer gave Joseph charge of the prison**

²² And the keeper of the prison committed to Joseph's hand all the prisoners that were in the prison; and whatsoever they did there, he was the doer of it. ²³ The keeper of the prison looked not to any thing that was under his hand; because the LORD *was with him, and that which he did, the* LORD *made it to prosper. (Genesis 39:22-23)*

God gave Joseph complete and absolute authority in the pit. This is an excellent example of what God will do for His people even in the worst of times. No time or place can dictate to us the power of God. God's power remains the same no matter where we are, how we got there, or what is going on. Joseph had no struggle in the pit – the jailer simply turned the keys over to him and he began his assignment in prison.

- **God gave Jesus complete authority over hell and death**

By which also he went and preached unto the spirits in prison; (I Peter 3:19)

I am he that liveth, and was dead; and, behold, I am alive for evermore, Amen; and have the keys of hell and of death. (Revelation 1:18)

God gave Jesus the keys of hell and death. He did not have to struggle for them. Not only does He have the keys of hell and death, He told us that the gates of hell shall not prevail against us.

- **Joseph interpreted dreams of two individuals in which one lived and the other died**

And they dreamed a dream both of them, each man his dream in one night, each man according to the interpretation of his dream, the butler and the baker of the king of Egypt, which were bound in the prison. (Genesis 40:5)
⁹ And the chief butler told his dream to Joseph, and said to him, In my dream, behold, a vine was before me;
¹⁰ And in the vine were three branches: and it was as though it budded, and her blossoms shot forth; and the clusters thereof brought forth ripe grapes:
¹¹ And Pharaoh's cup was in my hand: and I took the grapes, and pressed them into Pharaoh's cup, and I gave the cup into Pharaoh's hand.
¹² And Joseph said unto him, This is the interpretation of it: The three branches are three days:
¹³ Yet within three days shall Pharaoh lift up thine head, and restore thee unto thy place: and thou shalt deliver Pharaoh's cup into his hand, after the former manner when thou wast his butler. (Genesis 40:9-13)
¹⁶ When the chief baker saw that the interpretation was good, he said unto Joseph, I also was in my dream, and, behold, I had three white baskets on my head:¹⁷ And in the uppermost basket there was of all manner of bakemeats for Pharaoh; and the birds did eat them out of the basket upon my head.¹⁸ And Joseph answered and said, This is the interpretation thereof: The three baskets

are three days:[19] *Yet within three days shall Pharaoh lift up thy head from off thee, and shall hang thee on a tree; and the birds shall eat thy flesh from off thee. (Genesis 40:16-19)*

Joseph interpreted the dreams of the two prisoners. They were both called before Pharaoh three days later. Pharaoh restored the butler's position, but he hanged the baker.

- **Jesus was crucified between two thieves; one went to paradise and the other perished**

And there were also two other, malefactors, led with him to be put to death. And when they were come to the place, which is called Calvary, there they crucified him, and the malefactors, one on the right hand, and the other on the left. (Luke 23:32-33)

[39] And one of the malefactors which were hanged railed on him, saying, If thou be Christ, save thyself and us.

[40] But the other answering rebuked him, saying, Dost not thou fear God, seeing thou art in the same condemnation?

[41] And we indeed justly; for we receive the due reward of our deeds: but this man hath done nothing amiss.

[42] And he said unto Jesus, Lord, remember me when thou comest into thy kingdom. [43] And Jesus said unto him, Verily I say unto you, Today shall you be with me in paradise. (Luke 23:39-43)

Both of the criminals were guilty as charged, however, the differences between the two is that one believed on Jesus and the other did not. The one who believed gained everlasting life with Jesus Christ. As is true even now, those who believe are saved and those who do not are damned.

- **All of Egypt bowed before Joseph**

And he made him to ride in the second chariot which he had; and they cried before him, Bow the knee: and he made him ruler over all the land of Egypt. (Genesis 41:43)

And Joseph was the governor over the land, and he it was that sold to all the people of the land: and Joseph's brethren came, and bowed down themselves before him with their faces to the earth. (Genesis 42:6)

Just as Joseph had dreamed, his eleven brothers, his father, and mother bowed to him. All who came before Joseph in Egypt were commanded to bow the knee.

- **The whole world will bow before Jesus**

⁹ Wherefore God also hath highly exalted him, and given him a name which is above every name:
¹⁰ That at the name of Jesus every knee should bow, of things in heaven, and things in earth, and things under the earth; (Philippians 2:9-10)

- **Pharaoh gave Joseph a new name**

And Pharaoh called Joseph's name Zaphnathpaaneah; and he gave him to wife Asenath the daughter of Potipherah priest of On. And Joseph went out over all the land of Egypt. (Genesis 41:45)

When people came before the new Joseph, they were commanded to bow the knee.

- **God gave Jesus His name**

And, behold, thou shalt conceive in thy womb, and bring forth a son, and shalt call his name JESUS.
(Luke 1:31)

Jesus is the Savior of the world. He brought deliverance not only to Israel, but to the entire world. And there is no other name under heaven whereby we can be saved. *(Acts 4:12)*

- **Joseph was 30 years of age when he began his ministry**

And Joseph was thirty years old when he stood before Pharaoh king of Egypt. And Joseph went out from the presence of Pharaoh, and went throughout all the land of Egypt. (Genesis 41:46)

- **Jesus was thirty years of age when he began his ministry**

[22] And the Holy Ghost descended in a bodily shape like a dove upon him, and a voice came from heaven, which said, Thou art my beloved Son; in thee I am well pleased. [23] And Jesus himself began to be about thirty years of age, being (as was supposed) the son of Joseph, which was the son of Heli, (Luke 3:22-23)

- **Joseph's garment was torn from him**

And it came to pass, when Joseph was come unto his brethren, that they stript Joseph out of his coat, his coat of many colours that was on him; (Genesis 37:23)

- **Jesus' garment was torn from Him**

And they stripped him, and put on him a scarlet robe. (Matthew 27:28)

The people were sent to Joseph for grain

And when all the land of Egypt was famished, the people cried to Pharaoh for bread: and Pharaoh said unto all the Egyptians, Go unto Joseph; what he saith to you, do. (Genesis 41:55)

Joseph was governor of Egypt and was in total charge of distributing food to those who came from far and wide. Whoever came to Pharaoh for food, Pharaoh immediately re-routed them to Joseph because he was the man in authority of the food distribution.

- **Mary sent the people to Jesus for wine**

⁴Jesus saith unto her, Woman, what have I to do with thee? mine hour is not yet come. ⁵ His mother saith unto the servants, Whatsoever he saith unto you, do it. (John 2:4-5)

- **Joseph forgave those who wronged him**

And there will I nourish thee; for yet there are five years of famine; lest thou, and thy household, and all that thou hast, come to poverty. (Genesis 45:11)

Moreover he kissed all his brethren, and wept upon them: and after that his brethren talked with him. (Genesis 45:15)

And Joseph said unto them, Fear not: for am I in the place of God? ²⁰ But as for you, ye thought evil against me; but God meant it unto good, to bring to pass, as it is this day, to save much people alive. ²¹ Now therefore fear ye not: I will nourish you, and your little ones. And he comforted them, and spake kindly unto them. (Genesis 50:19-21)

When forgiveness is put into action, action is put into forgiveness. Joseph did not send his brothers back to Canaan deficient when he was in position to bless them. He proved his forgiveness by bringing them out of Canaan; else they would have come to a state of poverty as described above. Joseph chose to rescue his family from famine rather than watch them go down like those around him. This was true love and forgiveness in action.

Jesus forgave those who wronged Him

Then said Jesus, Father, forgive them; for they know not what they do. And they parted his raiment, and cast lots. (Luke 23:34)

We would all be doomed if Jesus had not given His life for us. Jesus forgave all who spat on Him, scourged Him, sold Him out, betrayed Him, denied Him, and crucified Him. We are free today because of the love, mercy, and forgiving power of Jesus Christ.

NOTES

ABOUT THE AUTHOR

Queen Kirkwood-Hatchett has a Bachelor of Science degree in Administration of Justice from Southern Illinois University in Carbondale, IL; a Master of Science degree in Public Safety from Capella University in Minneapolis, MN; a Master of Arts degree in Theological Studies from Liberty University in Lynchburg, VA; and a Graduate Certificate in Worship Studies from Liberty University in Lynchburg, VA. She is also a graduate of the Mega School of Theology in Cleveland, Ohio.

In addition to "Transitioning from Promise to Fulfillment," Queen Kirkwood-Hatchett is also the author of two other publications, "A General Study of the Books of the Bible," published in 2006, which opened doors for her to minister inside prisons, and "From the Heart," her first publication in 1994. Her most famous poem, "Crack, the Drug from Hell," from her first publication, opened many doors for her to minister to the hurting and lost in congregations, schools, and museums throughout northern and southern Illinois, Ohio, and other establishments.

www.ingramcontent.com/pod-product-compliance
Lightning Source LLC
Chambersburg PA
CBHW071135280326
41935CB00010B/1241